Where America Went Wrong

And How to Regain Her Democratic Ideals

Where America Went Wrong

And How to Regain Her Democratic Ideals

John R. Talbott

An Imprint of PEARSON EDUCATION

Upper Saddle River, NJ • New York • London • San Francisco • Toronto • Sydney
Tokyo • Singapore • Hong Kong • Cape Town • Madrid
Paris • Milan • Munich • Amsterdam

www.ft-ph.com

Library of Congress Cataloging-in-Publication data

A Cataloging-in-Publication data record for this book can be
obtained from the Library of Congress.

Editorial/production supervision: *Techne Group*
Cover design director: *Jerry Votta*
Cover design: *Talar Boorujy*
Interior design: *Meg VanArsdale*
Manufacturing buyer: *Alexis Heydt-Long*
Executive editor: *Jim Boyd*
Editorial assistant: *Linda Ramagnano*
Marketing manager: *John Pierce*
Full-service production manager: *Anne R. Garcia*

© 2004 Pearson Education, Inc.
Publishing as Financial Times Prentice Hall
Upper Saddle River, New Jersey 07458

Financial Times Prentice Hall books are widely used by corporations and government
agencies for training, marketing, and resale.

For information regarding corporate and government bulk discounts please
contact: Corporate and Government Sales at (800) 382-3419 or email to
corpsales@pearsontechgroup.com.

Company and product names mentioned herein are the trademarks or registered
trademarks of their respective owners.

Printed in the United States of America

10   9   8   7   6   5   4   3   2   1

ISBN 0-13-143051-3

Pearson Education Ltd.
Pearson Education Australia Pty., Limited
Pearson Education South Asia Pte. Ltd.
Pearson Education Asia Ltd.
Pearson Education Canada, Ltd.
Pearson Educación de Mexico, S.A. de C.V.
Pearson Education-Japan
Pearson Malaysia S.D.N. B.H.D.

Truly we have a great gross national product, ..., but can that be the criterion by which we judge this country? Is it enough? For the gross national product counts air pollution and cigarette advertising and ambulances to clear our highways of carnage. It counts special locks for our doors and jails for the people who break them. It counts Whitman's rifle and Speck's knife and television programs, which glorify violence in order to sell toys to our children. And the gross national product, the gross national product does not allow for the health of our children, the quality of their education, the joy of their play. It is indifferent to the decency of our factories and the safety of our streets alike. It does not include the beauty of our poetry or the strength of our marriages, the intelligence of our public debate or the integrity of our public officials. It measures neither wit nor courage, neither our wisdom nor our learning, neither our compassion nor our duty to our country. It measures everything, in short, except that which makes life worthwhile, and it can tell us everything about America, except why we are proud to be Americans.

ROBERT F. KENNEDY
JANUARY 4, 1968

CONTENTS

America's Problems at Home

America's Problems Abroad

Who Will Tell the People?

Summary and Conclusion

Appendix

America's Problems at Home

Revolutions are not about trifles, but spring from trifles.
ARISTOTLE

1

WHAT IS WRONG WITH AMERICA?

In answer to the question, "What is wrong with America?" some might have trouble finding any flaw while others would need hours, if not days, to begin to enumerate all the problems they perceive. Surely, America is not without faults. But what good can come from dwelling on or overemphasizing its weaknesses?

Physical scientists are currently searching for a solution to one of the greatest problems in the history of physics: a "unified" theory that will simplify our understanding of our universe by combining our knowledge of electrical, nuclear, and gravitational forces into one single equation. Some physicists have gone as far as to hint that when this work is completed, it will signal the end of science.

In the political and economic research arena, there is also a great effort under way to understand how the peoples of the world can better work and live together on this planet. There is hope for a global unified theory that might help explain a great deal about how people the world over productively organize themselves because many questions of economics and governance are the same everywhere in the world. Also, humans are much more similar around the world than we like to admit. We all want to live full, meaningful lives, we wish to make a contribution in our lives, and we want to be free. Why freedom and individual choice are so appealing to humans is beyond the scope of this book, but the desire also appears to be universal. Certainly there are cultural and ethnic differences around the planet, but "..., in the final analysis, our most basic common link is that we all inhabit this small planet. We all breathe the same air. We all cherish our children's future. And we are all mortal" (John F. Kennedy).

And so what is this common unifying force that might solve many of America's and the world's economic, societal, and governmental problems? It is greater democracy! By world standards, America is far from being the least democratic of the countries on earth, but examination of its current problems suggests that greater democracy may help solve many of its most intractable problems. Greater democracy in America means greater and more direct involvement by the American people in their government, a dramatic reduction in the undue influence of special interests that distort the democratic governance process and guarantees that the free press and basic civil liberties will be protected.

It has long been understood that democracy, at least theoretically, provides a country's citizens with tremendous individual freedom. Democracy, it turns out, also has a very important role to play in establishing and maintaining a healthy and prosperous economy. Economies grow when people invest in businesses, their families, and their education. And a necessary precondition for investment is good government that can ensure that fair and just rules are set as to how economic activity develops. It turns out that democracy's value to an economy is in policing the government to ensure it not only sets fair rules of play for the economy but that the government itself does not become coercive toward its citizens. So an investigation of America's problems is not meant to demean the country, but rather to uncover opportunities it might undertake to attain even greater economic and cultural accomplishments and restore it to its proper place as the beacon of freedom and opportunity to all the peoples of the world.

Many Americans today might consider it unpatriotic for their fellow citizens to publicly criticize the policies of their government. Especially in war time, it is commonly thought that good citizens should stand behind their commander-in-chief and allow him or her to speak with one unified voice.

Antiwar protestors during the Vietnam conflict were told that with regard to America they should either "love it or leave it." But times have changed. Different Americans have drawn different conclusions about how that war was fought; some hawks have decided we could have won the war if only we had let the generals fight it. Many Americans believe it was a mistake to get involved from the start, and many of those consider it an immoral war.

At the time, it was hard to tell which side held the moral high ground. Wars are always bloody events, so arguing morals in the middle of an essentially amoral affair is rather difficult. But with hindsight, most people now agree that the antiwar protestors were right. Dominoes or no dominoes, America probably had very little business fighting in a small country's civil war halfway around the world. Interestingly, anyone who visits the Vietnam Memorial in Washington, D.C., on any given day may witness a remarkable event—former soldiers from the conflict in bear hugs with former

Vietnam War protesters. It appears that even our former troops have come to appreciate the role played by the antiwar activists in getting them home safely to their families and loved ones.

During the recent Iraq War, the American administration again began to argue that any dissent or criticism of the government was not only harmful to the cause but a sign of disloyalty to the nation. To crush dissent during conflicts seems to violate some of the fundamental rights that America as a democratic nation fights for— the freedoms of assembly, association, and speech. It is during critical periods like wars that a democratic government should be most attentive to the wishes of its populace. Only the general citizenry can give its leaders essential feedback regarding their perception of the morality of the conflict, the acceptable levels of human loss and suffering they are willing to endure, and when, if ever, is an appropriate time to sue for peace. Generals, presidents, and other elected representatives are often too close to the operational aspects of the conflict and may have developed a "win at any cost" mentality, as combatants often do. Only the general populace can maintain a "big picture" perspective and properly weigh the true costs and benefits of the war since it is their sons and daughters who are being put in harm's way. Therefore, it is essential that the general populace be well informed by an unbiased and independent media and maintain a strong voice in their government.

Now, in the post-Iraq War world, one finds that the conflict is not over. It is said that the battle against terrorism has no finish line and that again, criticism of the administration harms the cause against the enemy. The FBI has collected extensive information on antiwar protestors in America, arguing in an FBI memorandum that it is trying to suppress terrorism. (*The New York Times,* 11/23/03). The use of the scare word "terrorists" to attack the civil liberties of people participating in democratic protests concerns many in America. It very well may be that the war on terrorism will be endless, but does this mean that Americans must forever cease their criticism of their government?

The American military emerged from Vietnam with a doctrine of not entering a new war without very well-defined goals, clear objectives, and a definitive time frame in which to end hostilities. And now, generals have been drawn into a war on terror that knows no country boundaries, has a very poorly defined enemy, and has objectives so muddy that it is inconceivable the conflict will ever end. As Secretary of Defense Donald Rumsfeld wrote in a memo to his staff in October 2003 concerning the never-ending Iraq clean-up operation, the U.S. was spending billions while the enemies, the so-called terrorists, were spending millions. He added, for every enemy we kill, hundreds more are successfully recruited to the terrorist cause (*The New York Times*, 10/24/03). If you agree that no weapons of mass destruction were found, Saddam Hussein had nothing to do with 9/11, and world opinion has shifted dramatically against the United States, it is starting to look as if the antiwar crowd was right again. If the objective was to minimize terrorist activity in the world, nobody better claim "mission accomplished" anytime soon.

So in the spirit of everything that is good and patriotic and democratic in the act of protesting and criticizing one's government, it is time to cry out that something is terribly wrong with America. Although the war is a striking example of this, this treatise goes far beyond the battlefields of war to examine a number of other problems in America. Those Americans who feel there is something wrong and say nothing are the ones who should be labeled unpatriotic. To see problems in America that are serious enough to cause her harm and do nothing is almost seditious, if the definition of sedition could be stretched for these purposes to include intentional inactivity in the face of an impending threat to the country.

Many Americans feel in their hearts that something is not quite right with their country. They see a wide variety of problems that are not being addressed properly by the government and wonder if something is fundamentally wrong with America itself. Much has been made of the government's inability or lack of desire to deal effectively with an extremely volatile economy, the lack of good new jobs being created, real wages that haven't grown for decades, our declining schools, exploding health care costs, a broken Social Security system, and poverty at home and abroad.

A third-party perspective might be helpful for understanding the depth of this problem, and polling people from other countries can provide that perspective. Researchers have found that 11 out of the 12 countries polled for both periods viewed the U.S. less favorably in 2003 than in 2002 (see Table 1.1). The only exception was Pakistan, which saw the percentage of its people that viewed the U.S. favorably increase during the period, but from a modest 10% to an underwhelming 13% (Pew Global Attitudes Project as reported in *The New York Times* 9/11/03). Without identifying potential causes, such a poll should act as a warning that indeed something has changed for the worse in America.

If you ask a variety of Americans what is wrong, they will identify several different symptoms, which at first appear to be the result of completely different problems. Upon further review, however, one can argue that these varying signs of decay are the result of one overriding issue—the demise of democracy. Such a statement is very bold indeed, because such symptoms of a sick society are very far-reaching and affect Americans at home with their families, at work, and in their relationships with the other countries of the world.

Various people would likely compile different lists of potential problems in America and surely would rank them differently, but an extremely important phenomenon is the feeling of many Americans

Table 1.1 Respondents Who Viewed America
Favorably by Country, July 2002 and July 2003 (%)

	July 2002	July 2003
Brazil	52	34
Britain	75	70
Canada	72	63
France	63	43
Germany	61	45
Indonesia	61	15
Israel	NA	79
Italy	70	60
Morocco	NA	27
Nigeria	77	61
Pakistan	10	13
Russia	61	36
South Korea	53	46
Turkey	30	15

Source: Pew Global Attitudes Project as reported in
The New York Times, 9/11/03

that they are all alone. As Robert Putnam has shown in his book
Bowling Alone: The Collapse and Revival of American Community,
Americans spend far more of their free time in individual pursuits
than they did in the 1950s. Americans used to spend many more
hours with other people, whether it was at their children's ballgames,
Girl Scout and Boy Scout meetings, religious socials, neighborhood
get-togethers, or even the local pub. Americans have become wedded
to their cars, and with both parents in many families working, there
is precious little time for people to attend, much less socialize after, a
child's ballgame. Their suburbs are full of big houses that they
retreat to each evening and from which they rarely venture out other
than to rent a movie or pick up some ice cream, again in the car. The
fundamental principle behind any successful community is trust—
something terribly lacking in America today.

An astute reader might argue that a weakening democracy in America, rather than causing these feelings of isolation and loneliness, may actually result because people wish to spend more time by themselves. Certainly it is more difficult to build and maintain an effective and cooperative democratic government if people do not want to become involved with others. While this is a possibility, the cause and effect in such relationships have a tendency to reinforce each other in a vicious cycle. Less community spirit engenders a weakening in democratic institutions, which further weakens the community, and so on. Change can most easily be introduced at the governmental institution level, so the focus will be on increasing democracy in hopes it has therapeutic effects on some of the ailments suffered in America's communities. If this approach is unsuccessful, more work should be done on Americans' desires to be alone. Fish rot from the head, and if Americans have lost faith in their neighbors, it might be a result of their first having lost faith in their governmental and business leaders. A more democratic, less corrupt, more deliberative, and more cooperative government can act only as a positive role model in inspiring Americans to get out more and enjoy each other's company more.

The next symptom that something might be seriously wrong with America also involves trust—or rather a general distrust of authority figures, especially in the federal government. The federal government is often targeted as the most untrustworthy, but many people are suspicious of all those in power, including state and local government bureaucrats, big company executives, bankers, lawyers, and even priests and doctors. Trust is essential in building cooperative efforts with government organizations, but if government fails its people often enough, the result can be an evaporation of trust in these institutions. Greater democracy is the key to stimulating greater trust in our elected representatives.

Americans are apathetic, or so they are told by their elected representatives. Indeed, there is data in support of this claim. According to the U.S. Census Bureau (November 2003), 50% of eligible Americans did not vote in the 2000 presidential elections. This statistic may be not a measure of American voters' apathy, but rather a sign of their refusal to participate in and support a corrupt political system. Again, greater democracy can help control corruption in a country and in so doing encourage greater participation in governing by its citizens.

Many Americans feel that their government is terribly out of touch with their immediate needs. They look at their job situation, their mortgage payments, their children's dilapidated schools, their long daily commutes through rush-hour traffic, their poor access to adequate health care, their bankrupt Social Security and Medicare systems, and the number of American families still living in poverty and wonder why their government doesn't do something. The government, it turns out, is doing something, just not for them. The government is passing income tax breaks for the richest Americans, eliminating the inheritance tax for the wealthiest, granting subsidies for big business, allowing the formation of monopolies and permitting multinational corporations to relocate offshore. By relocating, off-shore companies take jobs with them and avoid regulations having to do with minimum wages, work conditions, unionization, taxation, environmental protection, and worker safety. So it is not that your government is not hard at work; it just isn't working for you.

It is not lost on many Americans that corporations have become extremely powerful. Now that nearly two-thirds of married women work (Talbott, 2003), more Americans than ever spend their lives at the office, many working hard for big corporations. But corporations have moved beyond the economic arena and are now active players in the government. They are the biggest contributors to America's political parties and spend the most on lobbying the government (visit www.publiccampaign.org and www.commoncause.org). The Supreme Court in December 2003 affirmed a new campaign finance law, but it does not go far enough in getting corporations out of our government (*The New York Times*, 12/11/03).

It is a fact that America's wealthiest have gotten much richer over the last 20 years while its poor and middle class have stagnated. Real wages have remained almost flat for the last 25 years (Krugman, 2003). Trickle-down economics has turned out to be trickle-up economics. Besides raising questions about the fairness and justice of such a trickle-up system for this as well as the next generation, trickle-up economics also causes a fundamental problem in the way goods and services in the economy are allocated, especially those that everyone ought to have access to. It is much harder to support a free market system for delivering medical care if the richest fifth of the country's population has nine times the average income of the poorest fifth, which is the ratio in America (Roll and Talbott, 2002).

In the area of international relations, many Americans are puzzled about why their government ends up befriending, supporting, and arming so many dictators, especially as they inevitably seem to turn those same weapons back on Americans. America seems to be on the wrong side of the "dictator vs. the people" battle in many countries including in much of the Arab world, many African countries, some of the former Soviet Republics, Pakistan and China. Why isn't America the beacon of democracy in the world? Who benefits from prolonging dictatorships that are starving their countries' people and preventing healthy economies from developing?

Americans mistakenly believe that approximately 10% of the U.S. government's budget goes to aiding the poor and impoverished of the world. According to the World Bank, the real figure was less than .1% for 2002, and many authors have suggested that these loans and grants have harmed, not helped, development worldwide (Easterly, 2001). Americans are a very generous people. Why is their government so stingy with foreign aid and why is this aid so ineffective in helping the poor people of the world escape poverty? Here introducing democratic reforms might serve double duty. If greater democracy in America leads to greater involvement of its people, the world may find that Americans are indeed much more generous and caring than their government appears to be. It is also true that if more developing countries enact democratic reforms, they should grow faster economically and, in time, help their people out of poverty (Roll and Talbott 2003; this research paper is cited often in this text and is included in the back as an appendix). Perhaps aid to developing countries can be redirected to helping them establish good democratic and other important governmental institutions and then allow these countries to make their own decisions regarding economics and governance.

There is another troubling symptom that something is wrong in America. America's media have gone through an amazing transformation over the last 30 years. There has been a great corporate consolidation not only in the television industry, but also among radio stations, newspapers, and entertainment companies (McChesney, 2000). This change has undoubtedly resulted in greater operating efficiencies for the providers of news and entertainment, but what is the impact on the democratic form of government of allowing the free press to be controlled by a few, very powerful corporations? One of the cornerstones of any well-functioning democracy is a free and independent press. Has America sold its down the river?

To summarize, America has its problems. They seem to be getting worse, and they are not being addressed by the government. If ignored, they will fester until they endanger America and its people.

Before possible solutions can be suggested, the problems themselves have to be well understood. Then, and only then, can the
American people come to the necessary consensus to move forward
and institute real democratic reform.

The primary reform suggested here is a dramatic reduction, if
not elimination, of the undue and unfair influence special interests
have in the government. By far, the largest of these privileged
groups that should be restricted in their political activities are our
largest corporations. Their campaign contributions should stop
and their lobbying activities cease. The wealthy also have far too
much say in how our government runs. But there are other parties
that have too much influence in Washington, and to ensure that
every American's voice is heard, their influence also needs curbing.
Each of us is a member of at least one special interest group. We
are the elderly, we are environmentalists, we are union members,
we are gun owners, we are lawyers, and we are doctors. But first
we are Americans. Until we look past the immediate gains from
narrowly crafted legislation written to benefit our special interest,
we must ask the more fundamental question, "Is it good for America?" And once we learn to ask this question, we can ask the next:
"Is it good for humanity?" In this spirit, do not be offended if this
text attacks your favorite special interest; the book tries to demonstrate its impartiality and lack of bias by attacking every special
interest. Just remember that with an American spirit of hard work,
dedication, devotion, and cooperation, we will conquer these problems and put America back on the path to greater enlightenment
and fulfillment for its citizens.

2

IS IT THE ECONOMY, STUPID?

If you listen to the antiglobalization protestors outside any World Trade Organization (WTO), International Monetary Fund (IMF), or World Bank meeting today, you will hear a litany of things that are wrong with not only global free markets but also good, old-fashioned American capitalism. A few in the crowd are avowed communists, and there is a scattering of anarchists, but the vast majority are simply pro-democracy. They may come from various segments of the antiglobalization movement such as international women's rights, human rights, international labor, or indigenous people's rights, but they are almost all firm believers in the ideas that the people should rule democratically and that economic systems are created to benefit the people and should report to the people.

So how is it that a pro-democracy movement has found itself in conflict with global free markets? Both democracy and free markets were supposed to have led to greater personal choice and greater individual freedoms (Friedman, 1962). How did a political system like democracy ever get into conflict with an economic system like capitalism? Capitalism is supposed to be about pricing and efficiently distributing goods and services, and democracy is a form of government by which countries organize themselves. And if their missions ever do overlap, isn't it likely that they would complement each other since they both are meant to give the individual, whether voter or consumer, the most choice with the greatest protection against the abuses of centralized power? In a properly functioning free market, all decisions about price and quantities produced are made by the individual consumers and suppliers. In a democracy, final authority over the government resides in the individual's power of the vote.

To begin a discussion of why democracy and free markets seem to be in apparent conflict today, an examination, of what a supporter of completely free market capitalism might argue are the benefits of such an economic system, is called for. For these purposes, this advocate will be identified as "the libertarian" because the point is to convey how a free market might operate properly with as little government interference as possible.

First, the libertarian would argue that history itself has demonstrated free market capitalism's superiority to any other economic system; capitalism has created the greatest degree of wealth for those countries that have adopted it. Many empirical academic studies have indeed shown that per capita incomes are highest in countries with strong property rights and rule of law, two essential elements of a capitalist system (Aron, 2000). Daron Acemoglu of the Massachusetts Institute of Technology (MIT) has retraced 500-year-old data to show that those countries that had the best institutions to protect private property centuries ago were those that have experienced the greatest growth since then (Acemoglu, 2001). He makes a fairly good argument that the causality arrow goes from good institutions to greater economic growth and not the reverse.

If the polar opposite of capitalism is communism, the libertarian's case is strengthened because it is impossible to think of a single historic or current communist regime that did not degenerate into dictatorship and fairly low levels of economic output. The people of the former Soviet Union and Mao's China suffered enormous economic hardship, brutal working conditions, and terrible loss of life during severe famines. Although China is now experiencing rapid per capita growth, the levels of per capita income are still very low. Some are skeptical that the accelerated growth can continue in the future without large-scale changes in China's political and economic institutions, namely greater democratic reforms. In addition, much of China's new wealth is concentrated in provinces in the southeast part of the country, meaning that the vast majority of Chinese live on much lower levels of income.

North Korea is another example of a communist regime that has been in power for over 50 years and yet is economically bankrupt. It must appeal to foreign aid providers to feed its starving peoples and ask foreign countries to build its power plants to provide its people heat and electricity. Many Southeast Asian countries including Laos, Vietnam, and Cambodia are experimenting with various forms of communism, and all are experiencing very low levels of economic development. Contrast the dramatic growth of their more capitalistic neighbors Thailand, Indonesia, and the Philippines (Rodrik 2001).

Cuba has been communist for over 50 years and even compared with the conditions of its rather poor Caribbean island neighbors, its economy is extremely destitute. Costa Rica and Trinidad and Tobago have embraced free markets and have grown substantially (CIA Factbook 2003 and World Bank 2002) while Cuba's economy languishes. The few automobiles on the road are American roadsters from the 1950s, and those are owned by the luckiest citizens. After the fall of the Soviet Union, Cuba lost billions in economic aid from the USSR, and Castro's first action was to order millions of bicycles from China for his people (*Associated Press,* 11/15/00). Castro has suggested that the American trade embargo on Cuba is the cause of its slow economic development, and it certainly has had some retarding effect. But it is difficult to understand how Cuba could not grow internally or establish other trading partners to overcome this hardship.

So now emboldened by these examples, the libertarian makes a stronger statement: "There is not, and never has been, an economic system superior to free market capitalism for creating wealth in a country, maximizing the income and well-being of its people, and mitigating poverty." This seems at least partly true because it is impossible to name a country in any historical period in which average incomes on a real basis were as high as in the capitalistic countries of today. Certainly in ancient Egypt, imperial Rome, and mercantilist Italy there were wealthy individuals, but if their wealth were averaged across the entire population, the well-being and standard of living of an average citizen would be quite lower than it is today (Maddison, 2001). It is probably fair to say that if these historical economic systems tried to compete against free market capitalism, they would prove far inferior in providing incomes and wealth to their citizens. Karl Marx envisioned capitalism failing not because it couldn't provide; rather, he believed that capitalism would eventually fall under the weight of complications arising from its own successes.

One could argue that much of the difference in incomes between historical regimes and modern capitalistic systems is due to technological improvements. This is true because most of the earlier societies, as well as many of the communist regimes today, were primarily agrarian, lacking extensive industrialization. Much of the greater productivity of capitalist countries today can be tied directly to the implementation of labor-saving technologies and industrialization (Solow, 1956).

But how much was capitalism responsible for the development, introduction, and successful absorption of these new technologies into the marketplace? First, the profit motive provided the incentive for capitalists to invent and then introduce labor-saving technologies into the workplace. A competitive free market allowed these low-cost producers to displace older, more established businesses; one of the beauties of theoretically pure capitalism is its blindness to traditional power bases. The market just seeks the lowest price. Second, capitalism created an investment climate wherein capital could be raised to afford these new inventions. And third, the division of labor and task specialization that thrived under capitalism allowed companies to achieve significant size, production capacity, and economies of scale and to create a demand for newer and more productive machines.

Although it is interesting to speculate whether a communist or socialist state might achieve higher incomes today given the better technologies available, current communist governments have not availed themselves of this opportunity and are primarily agrarian societies. In fact, they are not only agrarian, but low-technology agrarian, depending on significant amounts of labor, unlike their capitalistic neighbors who use technology to create much more foodstuff from much less labor and land. The former Soviet Union and Mao's China tried to force an industrial revolution on their peoples during the Cold War, but they failed abysmally. People's standards of living were very low, there was great economic hardship and famine, and in the end, both systems collapsed.

What is it about communism that makes it so difficult to promote and sustain economic development? While the list of factors a true libertarian could give is quite long, at its most fundamental, communism depends on centralized decision making for all of its economic decisions, including output levels, distribution, and pricing. If individuals cannot own property and make personal decisions regarding its investment and use, someone else must do so, and that someone is a government official or government committee. There are two very big problems with this approach: It is inefficient, and it is susceptible to corruption.

There is no way even a well-intentioned committee of the people can make as good a decision about allocating goods as can hundreds of millions of citizens voting each day through the pricing system with their pocketbooks. In addition, history has shown that such concentrations of power are breeding grounds for corruption. Once a person has super-majority power in determining where goods and services will go in a society, those resources often end up in that person's house or garage. The tendency of centralized or concentrated power to breed destabilizing corruption through self-interest is not limited to communist regimes.

In the libertarian's bold statement, he not only spoke of capitalism's strength in creating wealth and accelerating growth in incomes, he also said it was the greatest force for improving the welfare of the people and reducing poverty. Even if one concedes that, on average, capitalist countries are more wealthy, how is this wealth shared across all the population? If all the wealth in a capitalist country resided in a few families' hands then one could not claim that the average citizen was any better off or that poverty had been relieved.

In fact, wealth is not shared equally in capitalist countries. In a free market system, there is no mechanism for ensuring that wealth is distributed equally, and the libertarian is glad there is not. The free-market libertarian depends on the freedom of the market to allow for various levels of individual effort, output, and income rewards. He recognizes that no free-market system will reward everyone equally. He knows that life is not necessarily fair and that some have "unfair" economic or social advantages, schooling advantages, intellectual advantages, or just incredible good luck that allows different people to achieve different levels of income under capitalism. The libertarian does not apologize for these differences; he applauds them. Such variances in income create, in the libertarian's argument, the motivations for underachievers to work harder and for the rich to invest the savings that will fund the next level of technological investment, leading to even greater levels of productivity.

It is not clear that a wealthy class is a requirement to achieve greater savings and investment. If the same income were divided across the entire population, each person could increase his or her savings rate marginally so that the total savings rate need not decline and total investment need not suffer.

Somewhat surprisingly, based on an academic study that this author performed with Richard Roll of UCLA's Anderson School, countries of the world with stronger property rights, better enforced rules of law, and higher per capita incomes, namely the more capitalist societies, seemed to have more egalitarian distributions of income across their citizenry (Roll and Talbott, 2002).

This finding flies in the face of conventional wisdom that says a higher-growth, more productive capitalist economic system invites large disparities of income. Roll and Talbott (2002) found no

Table 2.1   Selected Advanced and Developing Average Country Incomes and
Income Inequality Ratios, 2000

Country	Income per Capita ($)*	Income Ratio**
Advanced Countries		
United States	28,649	8.9
Austria	22,577	3.2
Canada	22,499	5.2
France	20,813	5.6
Germany	21,713	4.7
Italy	20,485	4.2
Japan	24,804	3.4
Korea, South	14,305	5.2
Norway	25,844	3.7
Sweden	19,519	3.6
United Kingdom	20,004	6.5
Developing Countries		
Bolivia	2,189	32.5
Brazil	6,647	24.2
Central African Republic	1,066	32.5
Chile	7,726	18.2
China	2,758	7.9
Columbia	5,886	20.3
Honduras	2,313	38.6
India	1,979	5.7
Kenya	993	10.1
Mexico	7,055	14.2
Nigeria	762	12.7
Pakistan	1,724	4.3
Russia	6,780	12.2
Sierra Leone	597	57.6
South Africa	8,645	22.3

* Data from 2000 in constant dollars.
** Ratio of richest 20% of population to the poorest 20%.
   Source: Roll and Talbott, 2002.

tradeoff was required between greater economic prosperity and more egalitarian distributions of income.

As can be seen quite dramatically in Table 2.1, the advanced world has not only higher average incomes than the developing world, but also, on average, more egalitarian distributions of those incomes. One can see that the United States has the worst income distribution of the advanced countries. In fact, in percentage terms, it is nearly twice as bad as the average for the developed world. People may be surprised to learn that Sierra Leone's average income per person is only $597 per year, making it the poorest country on earth. However, because of the extremely poor income distribution, people would be even more shocked to hear that members of the poorest 20% of the population in Sierra Leone earn less than $60 a year on average.

The idea that there is a tradeoff between growth and the fairness of the income distribution came out of the pioneering work of Simon Kuznets (1955). It now appears that whatever tradeoff exists quickly disappears in the very early stages of development as a country moves from an agrarian to an industrialized society (Roll and Talbott, 2002). And as Kuznets guessed, this temporary inequality of incomes may result solely from some members of society "industrializing" and availing themselves of more productive methods of manufacturing sooner than their compatriots. It is hard to imagine inequality not increasing when productivity jumps, as it does during a country's industrialization. In essence, for inequality to remain constant, everyone would have to embrace the new technologies at exactly the same pace. This is very unlikely in a free society.

The libertarian would suggest another major benefit of a free-market system—that it is self-policing. This means that inefficient and unproductive firms, companies, and workers would be automatically weeded out by the system. The competitive free-market pricing system selects for the low-cost producer and has little to no sympathy for the high-cost producer. Regardless of how big a company is, how long it has been in business, or who the chairman is, through its pricing mechanism the competitive marketplace rewards businesses that are efficient and productive. Firms that are deemed to be inefficient become unprofitable and eventually disappear.

At first blush this analysis seems harsh, but consider the alternative political and economic systems that continually reward old, technologically inefficient companies based on their political and business connections. Remember, with capitalism it is the market, not a centralized committee, that is determining efficiency. And the market is composed of hundreds of millions of individuals making decisions on purchases to maximize utility for themselves and their families. While bankruptcies can be painful to the employees of the defunct firm, in the long term, from society's perspective, it is better if they find new jobs in which their skills and talents can create products and services that are truly valued by other citizens. The free market's greatest contribution to increased productivity may be this creative destruction process that allows financial and human resources to move fluidly to productive ventures.

In a completely free market, individuals are not compelled or coerced to purchase or supply goods in the marketplace. Therefore, it seems sensible that if transactions occur, they must occur between willing buyers and sellers, all of whom must be benefiting from the trade or they would not have entered into it. In fact, there is typically an additional residual benefit that accrues to each, the buyer and the seller, because it is rare that a transaction occurs at exactly the price that represents the highest a buyer would pay and the lowest a seller would ask. So, it can be argued, that the benefits of free market exchanges are actually greater than those measured by market clearing prices.

The final argument by the libertarian on the benefits of capitalism might be the most disputed; namely, that capitalism turns greed from a vice into a virtue. Adam Smith in 1776 was the first to describe the "invisible hand" of capitalism in which all market participants, acting only in their narrow self-interest, maximize the good for everyone. For many goods and services that can be called "economic goods," it appears that Smith is right. In a bit of a tautology, economic goods are defined here as those goods and services that can be efficiently distributed through a free-market system. The definition will become clearer when we look at non-economic goods later.

To summarize, the libertarian has argued that free-market capitalism has created the greatest degree of wealth for its country's citizens, the highest level of personal incomes, the fairest distribution of those incomes that still preserves the productive nature of the economy, and the greatest alleviation of poverty in the world. Although many of these benefits result directly from industrialization, the libertarian argues that industrialization is most likely to occur in a free market society in which risk taking is rewarded and property rights are respected. The argument concludes by declaring capitalism has turned people's assumed natural greed from a vice to a virtue and that the self-policing nature of free markets preserves efficiency in the system.

This is probably an opportune time to introduce a hypothetical opponent to the stated positions of the libertarian, who is referred to here simply as "the antiglobalist." It will be the antiglobalist's objective to find fault with the libertarian view that completely free economic markets are the ideal system to maximize human welfare and well-being. While it is impossible to stereotype an effort as diverse as the antiglobalization movement, this hypothetical spokesperson can at least argue the shortcomings of completely free-market capitalism.

First, the antiglobalist agrees it is difficult to find alternative economic systems that have created as much wealth as capitalism.

She also agrees that communism seems to be a bankrupt concept. Still, the antiglobalist has not given up hope that there is another, as-yet-undiscovered economic system that will create the economic opportunities to allow every person to escape poverty and also do a better job of maintaining the human dignity and self-respect of every citizen. While the libertarian pins his hope of ending poverty on greater growth, the antiglobalist hopes for a more humanistic world in which poverty might be alleviated if the world's wealth were shared more equally. Finally, the antiglobalist hopes an economic system exists that doesn't measure all value and successes in dollars but recognizes many other human ambitions and emotions not easily captured in measuring the GDP.

Our antiglobalist does not agree that capitalism's distribution of wealth and income is acceptable. While advanced countries may have less income inequality than other countries of the world, many less developed countries are in effect corrupt dictatorships and therefore provide a very weak comparison base. America should take no pride in being more egalitarian with its income distribution than, say, Myanmar or Saudi Arabia. The world's countries average a tenfold difference in per capita incomes between their richest 20% and poorest 20% (Roll and Talbott, 2002), and she finds this unacceptable, especially given that in many advanced countries, the poorest are still living in poverty. She also suggests that talking about intracountry income distributions makes little sense in a world of international trade. Who cares that America's richest and poorest citizens are at a "reasonable" level of income relative to each other (The richest 20% in America make on average nine times what the poorest 20% make)? What of the billions of people in the third world who slave at starvation wages to produce the products and raw materials upon which America's economy is dependent? What is the difference between this national accounting system of income distribution that ignores low paid workers overseas and the way the early Egyptians accounted for the free slave labor used in constructing the Pyramids?

Although not insisting on perfect equality of outcomes, the antiglobalist sees the wealthy of the world sitting on enormous assets and savings while the poorest starve. Free market capitalism has no conscience, but people do. She believes that properly elected governments can interfere constructively with the free market on behalf of their people such that opportunities and outcomes will be more ethical, more just, and more fair than if the free market were allowed to dictate outcomes itself. She knows that this constructive interference must not be so blatant as to "kill the goose that laid the golden egg." In other words, government regulation cannot be so burdensome that it destructively interferes with the operation of the free market, and it can not be so taxing that citizens, including the wealthiest, lose their motivation to work hard and produc- tively. A fundamental difference between conservatives and liberals is that conservatives want everyone to play by the rules and ignore what results occur, even if all the money ends up in a few hands. Thus you can see why most of the wealthy are conservatives.

Obviously, for governments to play this regulatory role, they must be powerful enough to enforce any regulation or taxation scheme the people feel is appropriate. The government must also have the ability to apply sanctions to the offenders. Therefore, the question is not whether to make government powerful; that is a requirement. The real question is how to limit the use of govern- ment power to prevent the government from itself coercing its own citizenry.

Imagine the entire world economy is a roulette wheel and all the people of the world have a seat at the table. In a completely unregulated free market, one player could get hot and clean out many of the other players at the table. A good government, repre- sented here as the house, could ethically step in and, if backed by the players, demand that some of the winner's wealth be redistributed back to the poorer players at the table. You can see that the first requirement is for the house to be of sufficient strength to overcome any objections from the winning player. The second and more subtle requirement is that the house be so constrained that it doesn't steal everybody's money.

The idea that democratic governments elected by the people have the moral authority to step in and interfere with the operation of the free market is lost on most libertarians, especially when wealth or income redistribution schemes are discussed. I say moral authority because government action would be sanctioned to save lives or ease suffering of the people if it had majority support. If the free market economic game is played fairly, and some people start dying or the suffering as a result, it is time for the government to step in. Most annoying to libertarians is the idea of the government's imposing an inheritance tax because they feel it is an attempt by the government to grab assets they have already paid income taxes on. (In the casino example, it is as if the casino manager [the government] follows winners into the parking lot after they have cashed in their chips and robs them of their winnings.)

What is interesting is that libertarians do not like to admit that the free market could not function without government regulation and interference. Who enforces private contracts? The government. Who tries and sentences fraudulent company executives? The government. Who maintains the system of title and property records that the entire private property system is based on? The government. Businesses are very interested in having governments enforce patent, copyright, and intellectual property laws. Why should anti-globalists not expect labor, environmental and consumer laws to be equally well enforced around the world?

So the question is not *whether* the government will interfere in a free market but rather how much interference is appropriate.

Again, somewhat surprisingly, Roll and Talbott (2003) found in their research that the richer, more advanced countries of the world had bigger, not smaller, governments than their poorer neighbors, when government spending was measured as a percentage of gross domestic product (GDP). So, in contrast to typical IMF advice, one of the problems of developing countries is not that their governments are too big and need cutting back, but rather that many are too small and need reinforcing. As in Iraq recently, it is fruitless to talk about private enterprise development until there is a government in place sufficiently powerful to maintain law and order and create the proper governmental institutions required for economic development. One of the most difficult of these requisite institutions is for the government to have the authority to effectively tax and raise revenues for its own operations. The importance of a country's having good societal and governmental institutions in place before trying to build a private economy is best exemplified by Russia in 1994. The American libertarian free market experts were sent to Moscow to provide financial advice, and their recommendation was to privatize immediately. Without requisite institutions, the ensuing debacle created a private economy dominated by monopolistic oligarchs who stole the country's assets at pennies on the dollar and then operated their new empires through criminal coercion and fear.

Neither the antiglobalist nor the libertarian wants government to get too big. They both know that government, unlike the free market, has very few self-policing mechanisms and that programs run by the government often end up being terribly inefficient because of a lack of competition. But the recent problems on Wall Street suggest that less regulation is not always the answer. As revealed with the problems at Enron, Global Crossing, and Tyco, among others, U.S. Securities and Exchange Commission

(SEC) regulation is good because it attempts to ensure transparency of financial statements and prevent accounting fraud.

So the alternative economic model that the antiglobalist would like to propose is a free market economy regulated by and reporting to a democratically elected government. This is not a new concept; it is approximately where the United States was after the New Deal was enacted in the 1930s. What has happened since then, especially through globalization's opportunities for multinational firms to escape any one country's regulations, is a return to a much freer less regulated market system. Many of the advances of the New Deal have been rolled back, including unions' collective bargaining power, the ability of the government to effectively tax its corporations, the safety of Americans' pension and Social Security plans, the required separation of banks' debt and equity investments, and so on. Libertarians have now come out and suggested that the New Deal is what is wrong with America. In his new book, *FDR's Folly: How Roosevelt and His New Deal Prolonged the Great Depression* (2003), Jim Powell goes so far as to say that the depression was prolonged by the New Deal programs because they interfered with the free markets, especially for labor. Often, regardless of whether big business, big government or labor was to blame for the various economic calamities that have occurred around the world, working men and women have been asked to shoulder the major burden of the recovery process through lower wages and fewer jobs. Any economic problem, from a weak economy to bad investment policies to too much corporate debt, can easily be corrected by just lowering wages and waiting for profits to recover, if working people allow it.

Internationally speaking, many antiglobalists believe the major reason U.S. corporations move plants offshore has nothing to do with the theory of comparative advantage but rather they are trying to avoid taxes, find cheap non-union labor, avoid environmental laws, and duck government regulations regarding workplace safety and worker welfare (Greider, 1997). Globalization offers multinational corporations the opportunity to compete in an unregulated world where the only rules are written by nondemocratic organizations they control, such as the WTO. But as globalization proceeds, corporations have been allowed to ignore that economic participants must abide by rules established by a democratic government elected by the people. Corporations want no regulation, but the people of the world don't want multinational corporations running roughshod over them and their families. The basic democratic disconnect between free traders and antiglobalists is that once trade is encouraged between countries, it is not clear to which courts they answer, which multinational governmental body has authority to regulate, what democratic process gave that body its authority, and which citizens of the world it reports to.

Of course, the real danger in allowing one group such as wealthy capitalists or their corporations too much economic power is that they will cheat and try to use it to influence world governments. Maybe this explains why America has a long history of supporting dictatorships around the world. Simple, says the antiglobalist; it is easier to bribe a single dictator than an entire parliament. There is some truth to this. A bribe paid to garner access to a country's oil and gas reserves may be substantial enough to interest a single dictator, but it could lose its economic impact if it were divided among 400 parliamentarians. It also seems safer and more discreet to approach a single person than 400 with a bribe.

The antiglobalist is also concerned that unbridled capitalism will create a society that is morally bankrupt. Total emphasis on individual competition may engender a fear of cooperation and a lack of trust among the people. Without government regulation concerning child labor, might some corporations still be working 12-year-olds 80 to 90 hours per week? Libertarians mistakenly argue that not outlawing child labor is good because it gives poor families more choices, and greater choice is always good to a libertarian. The poor family ought to be able to decide for themselves whether their children work. The libertarian with this argument misses the fact that all poor parents, to compete for sustenance, would consign their children to lives of degrading work with no education and no future and at the same time drive wages and job opportunities down for adults. To say nothing about the potential abuse of children such policies end up being very bad in the short, and long term.

Any system that depends on extolling the virtues of greed for its motivating energy will create backlashes and side effects that it will have difficulty controlling. Rampant consumerism is a topic for an entire separate book, but pursuit of the almighty dollar has to devalue other pursuits, such as family, community, friends, culture, the arts and charitable works. As stated earlier, no prior civilization was as wealthy as America is today. Still, some people today would gladly trade places with someone from early Greece to have the opportunity to sit at Socrates' knee and learn, even if it meant more exposure to sickness and a shorter life span (W. Talbott, 2004). Not everything of value is measured in dollars.

Another major difference between the antiglobalist and the libertarian is that the libertarian considers growth good, not only because it increases earnings and stock prices, but also because it is only through growth that a society's poorest members will be able to raise themselves out of poverty. The antiglobalist is much more suspicious about unregulated growth. Locally, it can cause unmanageable congestion and pollution, and globally it can cause global warming as well as the depletion of the world's natural resources and threaten species diversity. It also can represent a peril to indigenous cultures and peoples.

The antiglobalist has one more serious issue with free market capitalism—there are entire classes of goods and services that it does a very poor job of allocating. If the government were not involved and the free markets were left to work by themselves, these very important goods and services would be allocated terribly. Remember, most goods and services are properly referred to as "economic goods" because the free market does a fine job of allocating them. Identified here are five other classifications of goods and services that the free market is ill equipped to handle: public goods, monopolistic goods, collective goods, ethical goods, and labor. Because the free market system does a poor job allocating them fairly, the government should be involved in allocating them. And because government will determine their ultimate allocation, free market participants bidding with dollars should not have undue influence in the government. This will become a primary reason to restrict corporations' and wealthy individuals' purchasing activities to the economic marketplace and to not allow them to bid for these services in the political arena through the use of campaign donations and lobbying dollars.

Public goods are those for which it makes more sense for the government than for any private entity to own, manage, and allocate. A typical example is national defense. The defense department has a very large budget, and its benefits accrue to all. Would we really want a private defense department negotiating with us about how much we would pay it to defend our families against foreign attack? What if we had to support three defense companies to ensure adequate and fair competition? Look at the recent deregulation of the electric utility industry in America. All the suppliers ran to gouge customers with increased charges, but no company thought to spend any time or money on maintenance of the electric grid on which the suppliers all depended. The electric grid might be another ideal public good.

Monopolistic goods are produced by industries that have a natural or established monopoly in a product or service, globally, nationally, or regionally. Monopolies are very dangerous in a free market. Businesses consumers don't like having only one cable TV supplier, businesses don't like having one supplier of essential raw materials, and corporate executives don't like to negotiate with one powerful national union. Monopolies have the power to coerce and force customers to pay an elevated price for an essential good or service. If businesses have very few suppliers—such as a single railroad providing service to a coal mine, one utility company supplying electricity to a home, or even a company like Microsoft taking advantage of its monopoly on PC operating systems—the government needs to step in and either provide the service or regulate it tightly. The potential for abuse is too great when there is no competition such that none of the self-policing typical in the free market is functioning.

Collective goods are so named because their ownership and sale fall into a broad economic category called collective action problems (Olson, 1971). In a collective action problem, the optimal outcome for all can be attained only by cooperation with the group rather than through the individual competition so typical of free markets (W. Talbott, 2004). Collective goods are the exceptions to Adam Smith's theory of the invisible hand. While, philosophically speaking, they are unique, in the economic world, collective goods are also incredibly important because their distribution represents one of the more important problems that a society faces.

It turns out that societies don't typically develop well until they learn to cooperate. Until they can establish a fundamental set of rules governing how business will be conducted and rewarded, no reasonable investor will step forward (Roll and Talbott, 2003). These collective goods require cooperation among all citizens and businesses in order for a society to achieve optimality by developing a system for punishing cheats and transgressors and rewarding those that cooperate. Providing these fundamental values that are the basis of a society and an economy are thus themselves collective action problems, and the rules instituted for their creation and maintenance become the first collective goods (W. Talbott, 2004). These rules include the theories of justice and fairness, a property rights system, the rule of law and order, the justice and courts system, the currency system, and even the rights to vote in a democracy (Roll and Talbott, 2003). Although economists often cite more mundane examples of collective goods, such as pollution, it is these fundamental institutions that are the most valued collective goods. Clearly, you would not want the free market setting the price of justice if you were falsely arrested and you were poor—although some might argue that is exactly what happens today in America given that the wealthy can afford much better legal representation than the poor.

Once we accept that these fundamental rules of organization of a government or society are collective action problems, we can readily see the need for a government's presence in these markets, for regulation and for a system of enforcement to penalize offenders. If such a collective market were not well regulated with strong enforcement mechanisms, "free riders," people trying to cheat the system, could always do better by ignoring the rules, not cooperating and maximizing their own welfare. These free riders come in many forms, including polluters, law breakers, property thieves, embezzlers, and even corrupt government officials. Here is the strongest argument that government must be allowed to allocate collective goods, why some government regulation is a good thing, and why businesses and individuals must abide by the law in a civilized society (W. Talbott, 2004).

Would you like to live in a society in which the collective good of freedom is not recognized so that poor people, desperate to feed their families, were allowed to sell themselves into slavery? Again, a libertarian might argue that legalizing voluntary slavery has to be a good thing because it increases the person's choices. The antiglobalist will counter that allowing such individual behavior degrades all of society, invites corrupt behavior on behalf of slave owners and traders, and violates the sanctity of the human spirit, which, we hope, is beyond being an economic good for sale in the marketplace.

Not all collective action is good. If businesses cooperate to the point of colluding on pricing or labor cooperates by forming a union that is so strong as to strangle all competition for wages, society is worse off. So cooperation can be good or bad. Unregulated cooperation or collusion in the economic marketplace is typically a bad thing. Unions, for example, can gain too much collective power if they are not properly supervised by the government. This may indeed explain what has happened in Argentina, a country with a rich history of union organizing. If the United States has gone too far in utilizing the free market for all of its allocations, possibly Sweden has gone too far in the other direction in overutilizing government to allocate goods that might be better priced and distributed by private enterprise. Absolute power corrupts absolutely—regardless of whether it is corporate power, tyrannical government power or even unregulated union power.

The next category of goods and services that are inadequately distributed by the free market is *ethical goods*. These are goods that the majority of society believes should be available to all people of a country because they represent basic human rights of individuals; no one should be priced out of purchasing at least a sufficient amount of the good or service. Obviously, the fundamental societal institutions described above, such as individual freedom, justice, human rights, civil liberties, and voting rights, would be included here because Americans believe everyone has a right to life, liberty, and the pursuit of happiness. The ethical goods category can be expanded to include a right not to be discriminated against and other basic rights protected in the Constitution. Other ethical goods and services include a decent education for our children, acceptable medical care for the sick, and adequate nursing care for the elderly. My brother, William Talbott, makes an excellent argument in the draft manuscript (2004) of his new book, *Why Human Rights Should Be Universal,* for why many of these ethical goods and services are basic human rights that must be respected by governments throughout the world. He argues that basic human rights are absolute worldwide and not subject to cultural relativism. Clearly, societies would not want these valuable goods and services being distributed by a free market based on dollar bidding nor would they want corporations and other market participants unduly influencing the government's allocation of them. As countries become richer it is only natural for the list of ethical goods to grow as people realize they can do more to ease the suffering of the disadvantaged and poor. Minimum wages of $10 per hour might be very sensible in America but such levels of earnings may not be achievable immediately in a poorer developing country.

Only a well-functioning democratic government has the moral authority embedded in it by the will of the people to decide how ethical goods will be distributed. Wealth itself is one of these goods. Even if you always play fair and never cheat, if you end up with all the chips at the end of the day and one of your fellow citizens is starving, regardless of how charitable you feel, your fellow citizens, acting through a democratically elected government, would be morally justified in taking some of your accumulated wealth and giving it to the disadvantaged (W. Talbott, 2004). Ideally, they would not tax you so much as to remove your incentive to work hard, and the poor would not expect such continued generosity in the future and quit working.

Labor, itself, is the final economic service that seems to be poorly priced by the free market. A libertarian would see the introduction of labor unions and the ensuing organization of millions of workers as a collective monopolistic interference in the negotiation of wages. However, this same libertarian may not see any incongruity in a million shareholders collectively forming a corporation and asking that entity to negotiate its workers' wages, one employee at a time. Labor unions developed and were supported by civilized society possibly because there was something fundamentally flawed in the way the free markets priced labor. Now as unions weaken under globalization pressures, labor markets are returning to being ruled by an unconstrained free market. Well, not entirely free. In China, workers are prohibited from forming unions, and union organizing there is a felony punishable by prison sentences of hard labor for 10 years to life.

What is it about the labor market that makes it different from other markets and possibly unsuitable for an unregulated free market approach in its pricing of wages? The market for a commodity like grapes seems to function fine, but the labor market for people picking grapes never has. The difference between the market for unskilled labor—that is, workers—and commodity markets like grapes is that even if wages head south to a level at which human survival is nearly impossible, workers must continue to offer their services so that they can feed their families. The grape farmer who doesn't like the current market price of grapes can change crops, let a vineyard lay fallow temporarily, build condominiums on his land or move to the city and take a manufacturing job.

One of the basic precepts of microeconomics is that suppliers of goods and services have the option at any price level to remove their goods or services from the market. Unskilled laborers have no such alternative. In the long run, they can improve their skills and face less brutal and fierce competition, but in the short run, they must continue to work and provide for themselves and their families. Unskilled labor is nontransmutable in the short run, and because people must eat, it will always be offered into the marketplace regardless of how low wages go. Under such conditions, wages of unskilled workers will end up at barely sustenance levels as long as there is a general oversupply of unskilled labor in the world. Although such conditions encourage the unskilled to acquire a better education and more advanced work skills, in the short term, such a free market's uncaring approach to humans seems severe.

One can understand why wages in unregulated non-union China average $1 per day (World Bank 2002). Often the employer recoups most of that with stiff charges for three daily bowls of rice and a crowded dormitory room. Why don't wages go lower? Owners understand that if they pay less, they will lose too many workers to sickness and death. The wage level is not set by a negotiation; it is set exclusively by the owner. For this scenario to continue, there has to be a constant supply of unskilled labor. Thus, it is important to corporations worldwide to pursue globalization, open third-world labor markets, open borders in advanced countries for immigration of the destitute to keep wages low, and encourage a high birth rate among the world's poor. The reason that the Mexican border is so poorly policed has nothing to do with liberals who wish to see Mexicans have the opportunity to improve themselves in America. Rather, it has everything to do with American businesses that want to keep wages low by continually introducing new low-skilled workers into the labor pool in the United States.

Where you draw the line between economic goods and non-economic goods determines whether you believe the free market should be unconstrained in providing that good. For example, possible market-based solutions to the overcrowding of the highways in many American cities are to impose new tolls or dramatically increase the gas tax. In effect, highways would become the exclusive enclave of the rich and middle class if the tolls were high enough to really discourage use by poorer Americans. Poor people would take public transportation or drive on crowded surface streets. There was a similar situation years ago when the rich flew on airplanes and the poor took the bus, but in this case, Americans may come to a different conclusion as to the overall fairness of such a plan. While Americans probably do not feel as if everyone has a natural right to fly on airplanes, they may object to having two classes of service on the nation's highways and roads, especially given that public dollars went toward their construction. Do Americans feel that all Americans have a public right to highway access, or are they comfortable allowing the free market to put a price on highway usage and, thus, deny access to the poorest citizens? Only the public can differentiate ethical goods and economic goods and decide which will be allocated by government and which by the market.

So the antiglobalist has made some compelling arguments as to why free markets may not be the ideal allocation mechanism for all goods and services. Although capitalism is an economic model and democracy is a model of government, the two systems are much more intertwined than typically suggested. The antiglobalist has also argued that for moral reasons, when the two are in conflict, democracy must trump capitalism. While unbiased, capitalism is nothing more than a mechanism for allocating goods, and its greatest strength, its lack of moral objectivity, is also its greatest weakness. Only the people, operating through a well-functioning democracy, can lend an economic system the moral authority a society inevitably needs to function smoothly. America has trended recently to an ever-increasing free market approach, especially with its emphasis on unregulated globalization, and because of this it has violated some of the basic precepts of how an economy must be regulated and organized to operate properly and maximize the welfare of its citizens.

It turns out that both free market capitalism and democratic forms of government are susceptible to corruptive influences in the real world (Mauro, 1995). Concentrated power tends toward corruption (Olson, 1986). In economics, it takes the form of monopoly power, and in a representative democracy, it assumes the role of a special interest. In each case, the powerful are trying to usurp a greater voice in the economy or the government than they deserve. A monopoly has more coercive power than its individual dollars might have in the marketplace, and the special interest has more influence over the government than is achievable through simple majority voting.

In summary, even an ideal free market economy needs government rules to ensure that the game is played fairly. While it is appropriate for a democratic government to police its economic participants and prevent coercion and fraud, it is a much more difficult task for a people to police government. There will always be some goods and services that should not to be allocated by a free market system. Because government best allocates non-economic goods and because everyone should actively participate in deciding how they are allocated, it makes no sense to allow anything but equal representation of all peoples when selecting one's elected representatives. Any system that allows unequal representation or undue influence of moneyed or special interests is therefore inherently unfair and non-optimal because of its inability to fairly handle the distribution of non-economic goods. Free market pricing doesn't work for non-economic goods, especially when wealth is distributed unequally.

3

IS GOVERNMENT THE PROBLEM?

One current democracy in the world has a particularly offensive anti-democratic record:

- History of subjugating women and minorities

- Government founded by radicals and revolutionaries using guerrilla-like tactics

- Individual freedoms and voting rights originally restricted to land-owning, older white males constituting less than approximately 3% of overall population

- Ninety-five percent of forestlands burned or destroyed by its citizenry, causing enormous environmental damage

- Weapons of mass destruction utilized during war

- Opposition to international treaties to limit global warming or try international war criminals

- Impediment to international free trade with huge domestic agricultural and industrial subsidies

- Economy in disarray because of corporate corruption and accounting scandals

- "Free" press owned and controlled by large multinational corporations

- Use of preemptive "first-strike" attacks against foreign countries

- Current leader seized office with assistance of highest court after losing popular vote

Of course, this extremely "undemocratic" country is the United States of America. Many people criticize America, and to America's credit, many of the most critical are Americans. America is more open and freer than most countries, but recently there has been a greater disconnect between our government's actions and the wishes of its people. Surely, this has not been lost on our international allies who watch us in a state of puzzled bewilderment.

Representative democracy has grown to be an enormously popular form of government worldwide (Diamond, 1992). In this third century of America, however, many Americans have forgotten what it is about democracy that is so powerful. Certainly one can recite platitudes about the individual liberty and freedom that democracy offers citizens, but our country's founders seemed to have a much better grasp of democracy's strengths and potential weaknesses than many Americans do today.

Primarily, democracy is a glorious tribute to the individual (Friedman, 1962). In an 18th-century world dominated by monarchs and God, America's founders drew on the writings of great

Greek, French, and English philosophers to create a government that celebrated the sanctity and authority of the people. People hold the right to control their own destiny; they cannot be ruled by governments unless they decide to grant certain powers to said governments to better conduct their affairs and preserve peace with their neighbors. All power comes from the people. No government can claim any moral authority unless it was duly elected by the public (W. Talbott, 2004). Although democratic majorities in history have committed immoral acts, to date, no one has devised a better way of policing concentrations of political and economic power than by making them obedient to a democratic government freely elected by the majority of the people. Actions taken by the majority are not by definition moral, but actions taken by a leader must have majority backing before they can be considered to represent the will of the people and be judged as moral. There is no such moral test or moral authority attached to autocrats acting alone; history has taught us they often act in their own self-interest, regardless of what their stated intentions are. Unfortunately, democracies have not figured out how to also guarantee the rights of minorities within a democratic society (Mills, 2003).

Our founders quickly realized the dilemma they faced in creating a government powerful enough to protect and punish, yet not so powerful that it came to prey on its own citizens. Their solution was to give the federal government very broad powers to protect citizens from coercion, but also to try to restrain it so as to protect individual freedoms. Any secondary school student can tell you they achieved this through a division of state and federal powers, a separation of federal power into three branches, and a constitution and bill of rights that expressly stated and guaranteed the rights of the individual.

Many Americans believe today that government has grown too big and that big government itself is the problem facing America.

In fact, as shown in Table 3.1, relative to governments in other advanced countries, the U.S. government is quite small as a percentage of GDP, and this data was collected before the two most recent tax cuts in the U.S.

Libertarians in the U.S. who wish to limit government power further might argue that our founders failed to put real constraints on the elected terms of our representatives, the size of government, its borrowing capacity, or its ability to run large operating deficits. But thanks to the wisdom of our founders, a procedure is in place for these good citizens to correct those oversights. Our constitution is amendable. The uncontrolled and unresponsive nature of government today is just another symptom of a more fundamental problem facing our country: Our democracy is broken.

Remember that one advantage free-market economies have over governments is that competition creates an automatic self-policing mechanism in the marketplace that governments don't naturally

Table 3.1   Government Spending as a Percentage of
Total GDP by Select Advanced Countries, 2000

Country	Government Spending/GDP (%)
United States	31.6
Austria	49.8
Canada	42.6
France	54.2
Germany	48.9
Italy	50.6
Japan	35.2
Korea, South	21.9
Norway	44.3
Sweden	62.3
United Kingdom	41.0

GDP = Gross domestic product
Source: Roll and Talbott, 2003.

have. To try to emulate that mechanism, and to make good governments more responsive to individuals and bad governments disappear, representative democracy was introduced. Just as individual
consumers set prices reflecting their individual tastes and needs, individual voters could establish a government that satisfies individual
needs and then police that government simply by voting.

The problem is that a representative democracy is as not as
easy to police as the market for an economic good like tomatoes.
Rather than require every citizen to spend every day studying every
issue needing government attention, the country's founders decided
to allow representatives or agents to do the bidding of the people
for them. Of course, they recognized they were granting enormous
decision-making power to these representatives, and recalling that
absolute power corrupts, they tried to make these representatives
responsive to the people by making them stand for election at regular intervals. That was 215 years ago, and then we went to sleep.

What has happened since to our wonderful ideal of democracy?
Forces outside of government have tried to corruptly grab power for
themselves. In addition, those good-hearted representatives we
elected have acted in their own self-interest to free themselves of the
bonds of accountability and have tried to consolidate their power for
their own selfish goals. This is the classic principal/agent problem in
which agents begin to act in their own self-interest rather than their
clients', but clients do not want to spend the time and energy to conduct the business themselves. Under such a system, it is natural to
assume that principals will allow a certain amount of corrupt activity by agents before deeming it worth their time to get involved and
clean things up. In America, now is that time!

A fascinating thing happened in America in late 2003. A popu-
larly elected governor was recalled from office after serving only
one year of a four-year term. Then-governor of California, Gray
Davis, was subjected to a recall vote, ousted and replaced with his

elected successor, Arnold Schwarzenegger. When the recall referendum was announced, many in elected government and the media called it a travesty of democracy. How could the people throw out an official who had been democratically elected just 12 months previously? Some even called the recall undemocratic because its motivation was to overturn the results of a democratically held election.

They could not have been more wrong. This may have been the most democratic act that has occurred in America since the civil rights marches in the 1960s. That does not mean that Schwarzenegger's policies are correct. But the people rose up against a state government that had presided over a tripling of their home electric utility bills, a quadrupling of their automobile taxes, the decimation of their school system, and the creation of a budget deficit that was more than 50% of the state's total budget for government goods and services (which was of course hidden from the voting public during the gubernatorial election of Gray Davis). As right wing political analyst Pat Buchanan likes to say, "Ladies and Gentlemen, it is time to get the pitchforks and head into the streets."

The world's press got hold of this story, and the coverage was incredible. At first the story's popularity was explained by the personalities and characters involved (*The New York Times*, 8/07/03), especially Arnold. But then people became fascinated that a state government could be overthrown by its citizens in the richest country on earth. Americans had never seen other American citizens rise up and in one voice scream, as characters did in the 1976 movie *Network*, "We're mad as hell and we aren't going to take it anymore!" Just when many Americans had given up any hope of reining in the power of their governments, the people of California showed them the way.

What was especially gratifying was that the successor was not a political insider; he wasn't from inside the beltway, and he wasn't even born in America. In what one can only hope is a precursor of future elections, negative advertisements about Schwarzenegger's personal life were totally ignored by the electorate. Certainly, Schwarzenegger's money and celebrity helped, but this was a very good first step at changing incumbency politics as usual, short of publicly financing campaigns. While one may disagree with the methods, one has to applaud that finally Americans channeled their pent-up anger into real political action.

Elected representatives in America have concocted a wonderful system over the years to ensure their reelection regardless of how unresponsive they are to their constituents. The most egregious component of this is accepting large campaign donations in exchange for political favors. These are nothing more than bribes, and they occur every day in Washington and in our state capitals. If not bribes, why would defense companies give monies to congressmen who sit on the defense appropriation committees. But many of our elected representatives don't stop there. They make it a near certainty that they will be re-elected and that their power remains absolute. They have fought against public funding of campaigns as it might eliminate some of the inherent advantages of incumbency. And in what must be one of the most unethical acts a democracy has seen, representatives have recarved their congressional districts through gerrymandering schemes to ensure that their biggest supporters remain in their district and potential opposition forces are discarded to someone else's district. Texas now has congressional districts whose borders wander about the state like a loose piece of tumbleweed (*The Economist*, 10/18/03).

Who are these outsiders who try to unduly influence our elected representatives? Perhaps Americans can regain control of our elected representatives by cutting off their supply of money just as doctors now are successfully killing tumors by cutting off their supply of blood.

We have created a new elite in America whose members have more control of our government than they should under a well-functioning democracy. On some issues, this well-connected elite is corporate America. On other issues, it is our wealthiest citizens. And in still other areas, it is large special-interest groups that exert way too much influence on our government.

What's wrong with special-interests forming to lobby our government to protect their interests? Surely, one can see the problem of a corporation's contributing $5 million in campaign contributions in exchange for a $500 million tax break. But is there a problem when citizens concerned about the environment gather their resources and contribute campaign monies on behalf of the Sierra Club? Isn't this the way average citizens make their voice heard in Washington?

What is the fundamental problem with special interests' exerting undue influence on the election campaign and voting records of politicians? Typically, wouldn't you want those people most familiar with a problem assigned to solve it? Wouldn't you want environmental groups focused on cleaning our rivers and air, teachers and school administrators straightening out our schools, and lawyers focused on reforming our tort system? Shouldn't those most knowledgeable about an issue and those who are most affected by a decision have the greatest say?

And what of the practice of special interests controlling candidates through campaign donations. Isn't it un-American to try to restrict the amount of money people can give to the candidates of their choice? This seems to violate the basic precept of individual liberty that democracy is supposed to be fighting for. Surely, no one can tell others where best to spend their own money.

Should dollars decide whose civil liberties will be protected or how our courts will be instructed by the law to determine fairness and justice? Aren't these issues that can be determined only by the electorate as a whole, with each person's vote counting equally? How can people claim their laws are moral unless those laws have been determined by a majority of the citizens? The sanctity of each individual in a society is protected only when certain ethical human rights are guaranteed, in equal amounts, for all. These qualities make America a free nation, and they are not for sale to the highest bidder.

This is one of the fundamental problems of free market capitalism distributing wealth unequally. Although the original distribution mechanism may be fair and ethical, the eventual unequal distribution of wealth leads to disparities in people's ability to "purchase" ethical noneconomic goods like a good education and adequate health care. The dilemma is that as wealth discrepancies increase, there is a clamor for the government to get involved in the distribution of more and more goods and services to ensure some for everybody, but government is very bad at efficiently distributing anything or even of policing itself. So as the free market operates, income and wealth disparities arise and more and more involvement of government is required to assure that the poor are not priced out of receiving basic levels of housing, food, health care, and education.

What about well-organized special interests that do not contribute campaign moneys but rather limit their activities to generating effective lobbying efforts on behalf of their members? First, no lobbying should be allowed on behalf of or by corporations because they are not people and they are not citizens, and the law should not consider them persons. They have been formed for business purposes only, but have evolved into one of the basic organizing entities for our republic and our lives. Governments should be concerned with the welfare of their people and only indirectly with the financial health of their corporations.

The world would be dramatically improved if the government were more concerned with the welfare of the employees of the steel industry than with the profits of the steel industry. There are enough business executives and Wall Street brokers who worry about U.S. Steel's profits. Certainly the welfare of corporations is important to the government in that these corporations provide jobs for the citizens, make products for the people, and provide them services. But the correct avenue to express these concerns to the government is through the people and the corporations' employees, not the corporate entities. Governments should represent people's interests, not business conglomerates' interests. It should be of the people, by the people and for the people—not for corporations.

To be fair, corporations might make the argument that they pay taxes, so they have a right to lobby the government. This a weak argument because many of the Fortune 500, thanks to their lobbying efforts to date, pay no income tax, and the average firm in that group pays less than 2% of its total gross revenues in income taxes (Talbott, 2003). But it would be a smart tradeoff for the American people if corporate America would agree to a repeal of all corporate taxes in exchange for a law that prohibits corporate campaign donations and lobbying. People would get back multiples of the tax they pay in wasted corporate subsidies, industry price supports, and other forms of corporate welfare (Palast, 2002). In addition, citizens are already paying the corporate taxes anyway in the form of higher consumer prices, which should drop once the taxation is removed. Corporations will never willingly agree to this trade because they are making billions through their donation and lobbying activity, and not just in the form of tax breaks.

Other noncorporate special interest groups such as the Sierra Club, including valid charitable nonprofit corporations, should be allowed to lobby, but not to contribute to campaign finances. Their money is the same color as the corporations' money, and it would only be paid to the representatives if they were getting something unfairly in return, even something as subtle as access to representatives. It is time that all Americans, regardless of the size of their pocketbooks or their group affiliations, have the same access to their representatives. If noncorporate special interests choose to lobby on issues that are near and dear to them, members of the general public should have the opportunity to have their say by forcing a general referendum on these controversial issues. Unpopular initiatives passed to satisfy special interests could easily be identified with government polls of the electorate and allowances could be made for them to be overturned by general referendum. The Internet is ideally structured for such a venture, but technology is available today to handle national referendums over telephones and cell phones. The days of special interests' deciding issues closest to them must end.

The fundamental problem with special interests' influencing government is that they confuse their self-interest with the public interest. Capitalism succeeds because it takes self-interest and turns it into a motivating force to advance an economy. While susceptible to the criticism that it is glorifying greed, at least capitalism has found a way to take one of the baser human instincts and turn it to some good; with industrial development and growth, many countries' populations have fought their way out of hunger and poverty.

The government has no such latitude. Because governments are in the business of allocating goods that money and power allocate poorly in the free market, allowing government to be unduly influenced by moneyed and powerful special interests defeats its primary purpose. Effective barriers must be erected that prevent moneyed and other special interests from interfering with the adequate and equal representation of all the people.

It is ironic that corporations and the wealthy elite choose to interfere in the operation of a representative democracy. It turns out they might have the most to lose, economically speaking, if democracies are prevented from operating efficiently and properly. New empirical research by Roll and Talbott (2003) shows that well-functioning democratic institutions such as voting rights, civil liberties, and freedom of speech are each highly correlated across the countries of the world with higher average country incomes (see Appendix). The research yielded strong evidence that democratic reforms cause economic growth and not that greater prosperity creates its own demand for better democracy. If correct, the study suggests that greater democracy is not a hindrance to greater economic growth but indeed might be a fundamental force in the promotion and sustainability of a prosperous economy. Rather than fight the pro-democracy protestors in the street with tear gas, corporations and wealthy elites should invite them into their WTO, IMF, and World Bank meetings. They should offer them tea and cookies and welcome them to a new alliance to expand world economies and conquer world poverty—properly regulated "free trade" and democracy.

Recently, the wealthy's steamrolling the passage of tax cuts through congress appeared to benefit them in the short run, but if society or the economy is permanently damaged, the wealthy could be the biggest losers. How short-sighted of the wealthy elite if, in grabbing $3.8 trillion of tax cuts in the short run (Krugman, 2003), they create a government deficit so big that it retards economic growth and thus reduces the value of their own stock portfolios in the future. The economy received a temporary Keynesian bounce due to the increased spending associated with the tax cuts, but as of this writing there was no pick-up in either long-term economic growth prospects or new job creation.

How do democratic institutions have a positive impact on economic growth? As mentioned earlier, a well-functioning economy depends on good government to enact and enforce a set of rules that is fair and just in order to create an environment for investment. Economists often narrowly define this investment capacity as corporate investment in new manufacturing facilities. But this misses the point as to how economies really grow. Economies grow organically, from the bottom up. This means that a healthy economy needs individuals and small business owners excited about investing in new product opportunites, expanding their businesses, maintaining their homes and investing in their children's education (De Soto, 1989 and 2000). Education enhances the total value of human capital just as building a new factory increases physical capital (Barro, 1991).

How powerful is democracy in stimulating bottom-up growth? When it is allowed to operate, it can be very effective. Raghuram G. Rajan and Luigi Zingales in their new book, *Saving Capitalism from the Capitalists* (2003), make the point that some advanced economies may have suffered from granting too much power to the biggest incumbent companies and industries to the detriment of entrepreneurship and innovation. In such an economy, big traditional businesses are prevented from failing by means of their hammer lock on government and industry allies (Shleifer et al., 2003). Properly functioning democracy will break that stranglehold of business on government by allowing the general populace to make the rules. Such top-down control of the government and the economy by powerful industry incumbents would be forbidden in a true bottom-up democracy.

Somehow, democratic governments have come to be stereotyped by some as inherently unstable. Nothing could be further from the truth. It is dictatorships that are inherently unstable; even successful dictatorships face the succession issue each generation. Dictatorships fight many more wars, both against their neighbors and in internal civil conflicts than do democracies (Roll and Talbott, 2003). Ordinary people, not leaders, have the most to lose in wars, so allowing those people to vote and choose their leaders is a natural deterrent to armed conflicts.

What type of instability do capitalists fear when they talk about democracy? They have a fear that greater democracy will lead to greater power for the masses and with it, a greater demand for "un-economic" property, land, wealth, and income redistributions. First, these economists have missed the whole point that some income and wealth redistribution may be completely moral and a positive development for the well-being of the economy, depending on how skewed income and wealth distributions have become. In trying to defend the sanctity of the free market system—namely, strong property rights and laws—they have failed to realize that a more fair sharing of economic and political power may lead to a more stable, more inclusive, more productive society. If a large percentage of a population feels disenfranchised, how can these citizens begin to feel excited about investing in that economy?

There is a second danger some capitalists perceive in full participatory democracy. Many people just don't trust or respect the judgments of other citizens. Even our founders thought non-land owners might lack sufficient intellect and motivation to understand and respect a government of the people and an economy that protected property rights. Today, many of us, even if we don't like to admit it, are intellectual, cultural, racial, or ethnic elites. We don't mind giving the vote to our own kind, but we are suspicious of those unlike ourselves.

The good government essential for investment and a healthy economy is provided in a democracy by virtue of having free elections; the democracy is self-policing and can be trusted to oversee the economy in a fair and just manner. Democracies are much better providers of good government than are any alternatives found to date. By good government, one means a government that is fair and just and that seeks to improve the lot and welfare of the majority of the people.

Democracies also police themselves by using numerous feedback mechanisms. A free press ensures that criticism of the government will be tolerated and heard. Rights to peacefully assemble and associate allow protestors to air their grievances even if they cannot get the attention of the media. Voting, of course, is the primary feedback mechanism.

A civil society's democratic feedback can be powerful. Antiwar protestors during the Vietnam War were instrumental not only in ending the conflict, but in driving Lyndon Johnson from office. The Washington Post stories on Watergate were major contributors to the downfall of Richard Nixon. Even simple published polls and reported public approval ratings often cause a reversal of previously stated positions by our elected leaders. While being accused of being "wishy-washy" or "blowing in the wind" at least these officials end up doing what their constituents desire.

Outside observers might laugh at the extremely vocal disagreements in the British Parliament or the Israeli Knesset, but it is exactly this kind of feedback and self-policing in a democracy that any well-functioning government and economy needs. Democracies often look confused and in disarray when they air their dirty laundry publicly in the press, but this organized chaos is what they should be most proud of. Tourists visiting autocratic countries are often fooled by how homogeneous the opinions of the locals appear, especially in their near universal support of the current ruler—it is not until after the revolt that the locals' true feelings toward their government are disclosed.

Self-policing in a democracy is important to many functions of a well-run economy. Clearly, holding politicians accountable for their promises, keeping them targeted on the electorate's welfare and needs, and protecting government against inefficiency and wastefulness are all extremely important. But the most important function of a democracy may be to limit corruption in government and the private sector. How else but with the constant self-policing of a democracy can any system of accumulated power be constrained to act in the public's interest rather than its own? Corruption is enormously hurtful to the proper functioning of an economy (Mauro, 1995). Contracts must be honored, property must be protected from thieves, courts must provide just and fair decisions, and legislators must act to improve the general welfare of the people (Clague et al., 1995 and 1996).

A democracy also benefits an economy when its electorate votes its pocketbook. If an electorate feels itself involved in its economy and democracy, it should want to support policies that stimulate growth and development. Equally important, an electorate concerned with its own pocketbook is more likely to support the economic reforms necessary to promote growth; namely, to encourage private property rights, limit corruption and overly burdensome regulation, promote the rule of law, and encourage a capitalist system of free markets (Roll and Talbott, 2003).

Milton Friedman (1962) said that a major benefit of democracy is that it limits the power of centralized governments. Just as a free market economic system removes much of the pricing, purchasing, and economic decision making from government, a voting democracy removes much of the political decision making from government bureaucrats. To the extent that centralized government is more likely to be remote from the electorate, is much more likely to have confused its own self-interests with the public interest, and is not subject to the discipline of the free market, the transfer of some political power from the government to the voter has to be a good thing.

It appears that one of the keys to controlling world population is democracy. The education and economic advancement of women appears to be the prime reason for the recent decline in birth rates around the world. Anyone interested in the long-term sustainability of the planet and its ecosystem would applaud this trend and realize that if greater democracy leads to greater economic opportunities for women, we all benefit. Unlike child labor laws that rightfully paternalistically protect youngsters who are incapable at their age of critical thinking, women benefit from having the option of working or not as they have no trouble making their own life decisions for themselves.

World opinion has shifted away from blind support for America. One reason is that America has done very little to fight for democracy in the developing world. Often, America has been on the wrong side of these battles, with American business backing old and tired dictators to ensure open and free trade. The finding that democracy is, rather than an impediment to growth, a major contributor to a healthy and vibrant economy might contribute to America's greater emphasis on democratic reform in the third world. American businesspeople realize that the development of the third world will open vast new markets for their products (Greider, 1997), but they have so far failed to recognize the importance of democracy in providing the stability and good government that are requisite for this economic growth (Roll and Talbott, 2003).

Democracy is important for both advanced countries and developing countries to prosper economically and develop truly civil societies. America, unfortunately, has witnessed a recent demise of its democratic institutions. If America can correct its own problems at home, then maybe it can once again become the leading advocate of democracy around the world. Through the exporting of democracy, we hope that America will gain the moral authority to once again lead the world and solve the greatest scourge of hunger and suffering in the history of humanity.

4

CORPORATIONS ARE NOT CITIZENS!

If the greatest harm to our democracy is the undue influence of special interests, then the biggest and most powerful and most destructive special interest is corporate America. Undue influence of corporations on the government prevents the government from operating properly, but it also results in unfair advantages to these same corporations in the private marketplace. Who would have thought that the one thing that is wrong with the government—undue influence on our democracy—would create the major problem facing the economy—namely, unfair economic advantage granted to the largest corporate contributors and lobbyists? If we can return democracy to the government, the economy should also improve resulting in the best of both worlds.

How is it that, theoretically, capitalism can be our friend and yet actual corporations are not our friends? Corporations provide a tremendous function in the business world as an organizing structure that allows seamless cooperative effort among many individuals of the same firm. Corporations also ease transactions with third parties that can rely on corporate reputations to honor contracts and perform work as promised. Further, corporations allow joint ownership by shareholders who can then effortlessly, and without interference in business operations, monetize their ownership positions by selling their shares in a free market. This system assigns market values to firms based on the capitalization of future expected earnings and creates enormous liquidity that allows resources to flow to those with the best available projects.

The problem with corporations becomes apparent when they enter the political arena. Some might argue that corporations are just like other market participants and should be able to be represented in the government just like individuals who happen to own their own businesses. There is even an argument that perhaps corporations should have more than an equal share of representation because they know best how to manage things, they control most of the productive resources in a society, and they hire the majority of its citizens.

Corporations should not have a disproportionate representation in the government. In fact, corporations should have no say in the government. They should not be allowed to contribute to the candidates, run political ads, or lobby the government. The simple reason is that corporations are not people or citizens, but to see the point clearly, one must examine their function and structure. Only then will people gain an appreciation for why corporations should be restricted from the political arena and limited in their actions solely to the economic marketplace.

Why are corporations naturally at odds with the average workers in the country? It so happens that the biggest expense item for almost all corporations, and the line item that depresses corporate profits the most, is wages. Corporations are in business to make profits, so it becomes one of their overriding objectives to reduce wages and eliminate unnecessary workers. Although this goal may be good for overall efficiency, you can see how it might not be the best thing for workers in the short run. If you believe, as discussed earlier, that the labor market is not a perfect economic market, then corporations' efforts to reduce wages might do enormous harm to workers. Labor unions, minimum wage laws, employee pensions, and employee health care plans might all suffer if corporations have undue influence with the government. A libertarian might argue that a laid-off worker's skills could be better used elsewhere, but this does not mean that the total cost of relocating and retraining the worker should fall completely and solely on that worker's shoulders.

What would happen if employees had a major, or controlling, interest in their companies? Employee Stock Ownership Plans (ESOPs), which provide employees with part ownership of their companies, were a test of this concept in the 1980s and 1990s, and many seemed to do quite well. The National Center for Employee Ownership (NCEO) in Oakland, California, found that a blend of ownership and participation helped firms to grow 8–11% faster than they did before their buy-outs (*The Economist*, 01/1197).

Of course, a number of ESOP's did fail, but it was not clear whether the cause was the large amount of debt required to create the ESOP in the first place or a problem with employees' motivation. While each employee was both a worker and a part owner, this arrangement did not seem to prevent any from conducting their shareholder duties to maximize shareholder value. Economic costs and human costs were nicely balanced.

In addition to working for corporations, American citizens are all consumers of their products. Again, corporations are interested in producing products at the least possible cost while consumers may be more concerned with product safety, product quality, and performance characteristics. Our interests are not aligned all the time, so it makes little sense to give the corporation an undue say in how government regulates products and ensures product safety.

Finally, some argue that what is good for General Motors (GM) is good for Americans. At one time, this might have been true. Henry Ford understood that if he paid a decent and living wage, his workers would be able to afford to buy his automobiles. But in a world where GM builds its cars and hires its workers overseas and yet sells them here, the economic link between what's good for GM and what's good for the American worker is much weaker. Even the profits of GM do not necessarily stay in America because its stock is owned by investors the world over. Should GM be able to lobby the government to make the import of cars from Mexico easier under the North American Free Trade Agreement (NAFTA) while American workers here at home lose their jobs? Surely America needs an intelligent debate about how much it wishes to open its borders to international trade, but shouldn't that discussion be led by its people and not ts corporations.

An astute reader might argue that the world would be more efficiently structured if run by corporations' owners than by workers. Owners care about profits while employees care about jobs. Corporations' economic influence need not be limited as long as it is constrained by appropriate antitrust laws and other appropriate regulations because corporations have indeed been great agents of economic wealth creation. But in the world of politics and government, their accumulated power has no place.

The primary reason that corporations' influence must be constrained to the economic business arena and prohibited from affecting our political and governmental institutions is that corporations are, by definition, economic animals. Their charters, their bylaws, the commercial code, and judicial precedence have all established that the sole purpose and responsibility of a public corporation, its executives, and its board of directors is to maximize its share price (Hillman and Keim, 2001). Maximizing shareholder value encompasses many valuable economic benefits—such as maximizing profits, cash flow, and growth prospects as well as minimizing risk, but these are solely economic terms that may or may not improve the well-being of the overall citizenry. In a speech at Loyola University of Chicago, Roberto Goizueta, the former CEO of Coca Cola, argued that business has a role in creating a "civil society" in which social ills are successfully addressed *(U.S. News and World Report, 6/9/97)*.

It is fine that corporations as business entities seek to maximize profits and growth, but there is no corollary that says these goals alone will make society better off or that they should become society's overreaching goals and objectives. Economic prosperity is an important component of society's ability to provide for its citizens' well-being, but it is just one way to measure that well-being. Clearly there are others. Peace is an obvious goal of most individuals in a society, but it runs counter to the profit-maximizing goals of a defense contractor. It's not that defense contractors would start a war to sell more arms, but their self-interest may push them to favor violent resolutions to conflicts that might otherwise be resolved peacefully.

The joy that an individual experiences from family life can never be measured in terms of corporate profits. The love of family and children is clearly a benefit not captured in any stock price. And yet corporations can ask their employees to work longer

hours, sacrificing time with their families. Should these corporations have a disproportionate voice in our government in deciding
required overtime or marital leave policies?

People take great joy in the arts and culture. Must museums be
profitable to demonstrate their value to society? Is the worth of a
Picasso captured solely in its resale value?

Finally, as discussed in Chapter 2, there are a large number of
non-economic goods and services that corporations acting as participants in the free market do a poor job of allocating fairly. This
is but another reason that corporations must be limited in their
control of the government. To allow them access to the government gives these purely economic animals influence over how non-
economic goods are distributed by the government.

The reason that individuals should participate in government
and corporations should not is that corporations, by their very
bylaws, are restricted to thinking very narrowly about problems.
They weigh only the economic consequences because that is what
they were structured to do. Although this narrowing of their focus
has been incredibly successful in the economic arena, it is their fatal
flaw when it comes to politics and government. For example, it
probably would be a good idea if corporations were restricted in
the amount of community support they can give. Should corporations decide who merits support and make charitable donations on
our behalf? Wouldn't it be better if they returned the money to
shareholders as dividends and allowed those shareholders to make
whatever donations they wanted to make to the organizations they
chose? Let corporations focus on what they do best: conduct business efficiently and profitably.

Corporations' necessarily narrow economic focus is also a
handicap in the area of politics. The goals of political and social
institutions are much broader and more far reaching than just
maximizing economic good. How can a corporation think about

the non-economic consequences of its lobbying activities when its own charter prohibits it from thinking of anything but economic reality? Issues such as quality of life, stress levels, family and friends, the home environment, health of the family, educational opportunities, and even the fairness and justness of the corporation's actions are all meaningless to a corporation actively involved in lobbying.

If corporations are given a voice in the government, the government is saying that economic matters are the only areas of import. Wouldn't it be much better to allow rational individual citizens, who are not artificially constrained by any corporate charters or bylaws to think solely about economics, be the agents who lobby their government for change? Yes, many of these individuals are employees of corporations, but you have to assume they wouldn't push for higher wages if it meant bankrupting the firm.

In addition to corporations' narrow economic focus, a primary difference between humans and corporations is that humans have the capacity for compassion and sympathy. When was the last time you heard a corporation called sympathetic? Even if the individual executives are sympathetic, their own charter would prevent their acting in any way but in the corporation's own greedy self-interest to maximize its own shareholder value.

Compassion and sympathy are extremely important in government affairs because a great deal of government's work is deciding how to treat the less fortunate: the elderly, the sick, the dying, the orphaned, and the poor. Remember that the people in a properly functioning democracy have reserved for government only those decisions that are poorly handled by the free market. How could a corporation make these decisions? When a government is deciding issues of fairness and justice, what possible input could an amoral corporation have? In structuring rules of law and rights of property, why would a corporation suggest anything fair and reasonable to the entire society when it could easily jimmy the rules to increase its own profits?

No, a major role of government is to decide issues of fairness and justice, to establish fair rules, and to compassionately care for its less fortunate citizens. Corporations are poorly equipped to deal with any of these issues, and if asked to or given the opportunity to lobby the government, they will do what they were set up to do, which is try to bend the rules to increase their economic advantage. Corporations are amoral and competitive by their very nature. This is exactly why they are so successful economically and why it is inappropriate to ask them to participate in government affairs.

We need not guess what favors corporations would ask for if given the opportunity to contribute monies to politicians and lobby them for favors. The written record exists. The U.S. has had an open policy of allowing hard and soft money contributions from corporations for years, and corporate lobbyists have always been welcome in Washington. The current challenges to existing campaign finance laws are based on the theory that a corporation wouldn't give money to a politician if it didn't expect something in return. As you might expect, first on their wish list is tax relief.

As Table 4.1 shows, one of the best investments a corporate CEO can make is the funding of a campaign contribution in exchange for tax relief. The numbers in the table are mind boggling. On average, the typical investment dollar spent on funding a politician's campaign or political party is returned over 360-fold in reduced taxes. While these are some of the worst transgressors, a typical company on this list made an average donation of $3.6 million and received tax breaks equal to about $1.3 billion. If you could make investments with that kind of return, you would make

Table 4.1 Corporate Campaign Contributions and Tax Breaks by Company, 1996–1998

Company	Campaign Contributions ($)°	Tax Breaks ($)	Hypothetical Return on Investment
WestPoint Stevens	11,100	121,000,000	10,900x
Colgate Palmolive Co.	63,650	286,000,000	4,493x
IBM Corp.	909,429	2,182,000,000	2,399x
Intel Corp.	869,991	1,288,000,000	1,480x
First Union Corp.	2,157,550	2,847,000,000	1,319x
DuPont Co.	1,192,942	1,515,000,000	1,269x
Saks Inc.	105,425	118,000,000	1,119x
General Electric	6,213,841	6,935,000,000	1,116x
Ford Motor Company	3,439,505	3,622,000,000	1,053x
Merck & Co.	2,164,907	2,222,000,000	1,026x
Johnson & Johnson	1,427,490	1,324,000,000	927x
Owens & Minor, Inc.	29,850	26,000,000	871x
Eaton Corp.	405,585	331,000,000	816x
Caremark RX Inc.	84,800	68,000,000	801x
American Home Products	2,129,449	1,401,000,000	657x
Lyondell Chemical	338,650	162,000,000	478x
McKesson Corp.	331,550	156,000,000	470x
Phillips Petroleum	1,398,541	653,000,000	466x
Tosco Corp.	436,616	200,000,000	458x
Burlington Northern Sante Fe Corp	3,158,085	1,394,000,000	441x
Goodyear Tire & Rubber	672,999	295,000,000	438x
PepsiCo	3,456,476	1,453,000,000	420x
ExxonMobil Corp.	5,625,761	2,312,000,000	411x

Table 4.1 Corporate Campaign Contributions and Tax Breaks by Company, 1996–1998 *(Continued)*

Company	Campaign Contributions ($)*	Tax Breaks ($)	Hypothetical Return on Investment
Verizon Communications	10,181,392	4,023,000,000	395x
Chevron Texaco Corp	6,984,355	2,474,000,000	354x
Weyerhaeuser Co.	1,202,543	419,000,000	348x
Ryder System Inc.	577,898	201,000,000	348x
Bristol-Myers Squibb	4,763,333	1,603,000,000	337x
J.P. Morgan Chase & Co.	6,764,038	1,917,000,000	283x
Microsoft Corporation	7,299,701	2,052,000,000	281x
General Motors	4,576,723	1,163,000,000	254x
WorldCom Inc.	6,224,967	1,313,000,000	211x
El Paso Energy Corp.	1,578,132	322,000,000	204x
AT&T	13,528,892	2,550,000,000	188x
Pfizer Inc.	5,748,614	1,074,000,000	187x
Walt Disney Co.	6,489,362	1,177,000,000	181x
SBC Communications	8,104,487	1,242,000,000	153x
CSX Corp.	4,825,072	562,000,000	116x
Northrop Grumman	3,639,016	408,000,000	112x
Phillip Morris	15,308,299	1,475,000,000	96x
Enron Corp.	5,691,893	284,000,000	50x
Totals	150,112,909	55,170,000,000	
Averages	3,661,290	1,345,609,756	368x

* Includes PAC donations, contributions to individuals over $200 and soft money contributions.
Source: Raw data and calculation of theoretical tax breaks from www.publiccampaign.org

Warren Buffet look like a "piker." Three hundred sixty times your investment, every year, is a 36,000% annual return, which not bad when Treasury securities are yielding 3.7%. Although this is a very rough study with less than perfect information about how much more each of these companies actually would pay in taxes under a different, more fair tax scheme, it does suggest the magnitude of the problem. Clearly, this analysis makes some simplifying assumptions as not every dollar of campaign contribution is geared solely toward achieving tax relief.

In addition to specific tax deductions like accelerated depreciation, corporations receive enormous tax subsidies—literally direct payments from the federal government. According to Palast (2002), they can also receive these other benefits in addition to tax advantages:

- Price support help

- Tariff protection

- A granting or preservation of monopoly status

- Import protection

- Liberal export policies

- Favorable regulations passed

- Relief from onerous environmental laws

- Restrictions on mandatory employee benefits

- Pension funding relief

- Liability protection

- A supportive government when it comes time to fight workers' rights to unionize

To put the value of these "softer" benefits in perspective, let's examine just the last one, the ease with which workers might be able to unionize. The percentage of private sector wage and salary workers who are unionized in this country has dropped dramatically during the last 50 years from over 35% to approximately 10% (U.S. Bureau of Labor Statistics). There are many reasons for this decline, but a contributing factor may be the laws regulating union organizing and the regulatory difficulties involved in setting up a union shop (Keith Kelleher of the SEIU, 2000). The laws were changed in favor of management in the 1950s, and union participation percentages have been declining ever since. It is not a coincidence that union organizing became a much more legally challenging task during a period in which corporate America dramatically stepped up its lobbying and election donation efforts in Washington.

It is in corporations' interests to limit the power of unions. Imagine, hypothetically, that an anti-union corporate lobbying effort in Washington resulted in a decline of $1 per hour in real wages for all workers in the country. It seems reasonable to assume that non-union workers might suffer any wage decline suffered by union workers as their pay often tracks that of union workers in any particular industry. It turns out that real wages have indeed stagnated during the last 25 years, with little to no real increase at all during the period (U.S. Bureau of Labor Statistics).

If corporations were able to accomplish this assumed $1 decrease in wages (or if they have accomplished it already), it represents an enormous transfer of wealth from workers to shareholders of large corporations. There are approximately 140 million workers in this country (U.S. Census Bureau) working 36 hours a week on average (U.S. Bureau of Labor Statistics). This means a $1 per hour cut in all wages represents over $250 billion per year savings to all corporations (assuming for this rough estimation that everybody works for a corporation).

This savings dwarfs the cumulative tax savings of $55 billion shown in Table 4.1. In addition, if these annual pretax cost savings (which are almost the same as after-tax savings because many corporations in the U.S pay no federal income tax) were capitalized at an assumed average stock market multiple of 15 times, their theoretical market capitalizations might increase by as much as $2.7 trillion. This $3.7 trillion represents no new wealth—just a shift from employees' pockets to shareholders' stock values. It would, however, cause an increase of approximately 25% in the value of the entire stock market. What many people do not realize is that the stock market captures the values due shareholders but ignores whether these values are newly created from an exciting new product or merely a transfer of wealth from another constituency such as the employees to the shareholders. Clearly, it pays to lobby your representatives in Washington. Do you think this might explain a major portion of the bull market during the Reagan era, which was decidedly anti-union right from the start? Remember, stock markets increasing in value say nothing about the condition or welfare of the respective workers or citizens.

When people make judgments about whether corporations and wealthy individuals are fairly earning their profits, they must remember that profits are highly dependent on the rules of the game. Many libertarians believe there is something natural or God-given about free markets and the rules currently governing them. This is not true. Not that the rules are arbitrary, but they are very much subject to influence and revision. To see the point, ask a libertarian why there are patent laws and then ask whether patents should be protected for 17 years, 40 years, or forever. Rather than being arbitrary, the proper patent life should maximize innovation by protecting inventors, but not act as a constraint in the long term on the distribution of new technologies beneficial to mankind. Having seen multinational pharmaceutical companies' reluctance to make AIDS drugs available to the developing world should convince the reader that corporations are not the best judges of societal and civic responsibility.

Give me one hour in Washington, and I could change the rules by which the economic game is played such that corporate profitability either went to zero or doubled, depending solely on how I fixed the laws of commerce. It is extremely important that all citizens have great confidence that the rules are being set fairly and justly and, yes, morally as well. Without this confidence, average citizens will not have the incentive to put their own capital at risk and invest in the game. If the rules were not fair, who would ever want to play the game and invest time and money? But without new investment dollars, the game is over. That is why it is critical that corporations not be allowed to influence how these rules are written. If Americans continue to allow corporate influence in Washington, they have themselves to blame when corporations use that power to grab more than their fair share of the economic pie. And Americans will have created the means by which the government sacrifices all quality of life and fairness issues in a constant effort to keep the corporate "fat cats" happy.

Table 4.2 gives an overview of what the biggest campaign contributing industries might be trying to get in return for their campaign contributions in Washington in addition to basic tax relief, which is pretty much assumed.

Table 4.2 Soft Money Contributions by Industry, 1999–2000

1. Securities & Investments $45,234,255

In favor of privatizing Social Security, receiving less supervision from SEC and government agencies, maintaining current dispute settlement procedure with investors through industry arbitrator rather than courts, receiving favorable tax treatment for their investors and their investment banking corporate clients, avoiding regulation of brokerage business, maintaining research business in-house regardless of potential conflicts, and deflecting investigation of initial public offering share placement business and their complicity in marketing tax and accounting schemes to corporations.

2. All Labor Unions $32,812,181

Against free trade agreements, in favor of subsidies for steel and other industries, desire raise in minimum wage, want greater protection against job-related accidents, and want union organizing regulations simplified.

3. Telecommunications $26,810,568

Long distance companies want access to local telecommunications, and wireless companies want to increase their spectrum at the expense of defense and education. Many are trying to protect local monopolies.

4. Real Estate $26,029,832

Maintain anticompetitive 6% standard commission on residential real estate sales, keep banks out of home brokerage business, preserve Fannie Mae and Freddie Mac's implied government guarantee, eliminate estate tax on inherited real estate, and keep mortgage business relatively unregulated.

5. Computers & Electronics $24,544,292

Received R&D tax break in 2001, pushing to allow industry to regulate itself with regard to Internet privacy, pushed to have China enter WTO, favor an easing up on prosecution of Microsoft for monopolistic behavior.

6. Lawyers $22,512,615

Trial lawyers make up over 80% of this total, and they are very interested in making sure punitive damage awards are not limited and that their fees are not constrained.

7. Entertainment & Media $19,406,361

Concerned with Internet piracy of music and copyright infringement of music CDs and DVDs. Fighting against restrictions on violence and sex in music and film. Protecting their industry positions in any shakeup due to new cyber delivery of media. Increased the number of radio and television stations one company can own in each media market in 2003.

8. Pharmaceuticals & Medical Supplies $17,471,853

Prescription drug companies want no investigation of possible kickback schemes with doctors. Want patent lives of new drugs extended. Prevent competition from generics. Prevent third world from violating patents. Prevent investigation of doctor and lab billing procedures.

9. Insurance $15,781,586

Prevent investigation of industry that is typically quick to collect premiums and slow to pay off policy losses.

10. Oil & Gas $15,495,655

Want to open Alaska and California coast to drilling. Want to do drilling and pipeline business with dictatorships around world. Want to stop any talk about research on alternative energy. Want U.S. to avoid signing Kyoto Protocol on global warming.

11. Transportation $14,209,432

Airlines want bailout with taxpayer money and protection of local monopolies. Trucking wants Interstate Commerce

Commission (ICC) to act as barrier to competition. Railroads want to preserve local monopoly pricing.

12. **Banks & Lenders** $13,287,562

    Wish to overhaul bankruptcy laws, making it more difficult for individuals to claim bankruptcy. Oppose predatory lending restrictions on charging exorbitant fees and interest on low-income families. Preserve onerous and hidden transaction fees for ATMs and bank transactions.

13. **Manufacturing** $11,633,494

    Keep as much of country as possible non-union. "Free to work" states encouraged. Make union organizing painstaking and time consuming in courts. Keep employee accident liability and Occupational Safety and Health Administration (OSHA) involvement minimized. Open borders key to offshore sourcing, but at the same time keep protective tariff barriers for select industries.

14. **Electric Utilities** $10,135,888

    Keep nuclear plants operating, allow older coal plants to retrofit without environmental improvements, minimize regulation of fossil pollution, with no requirement to explore solar and other alternative energy sources. Privatize but maintain local monopolies. Prevent co-gen facilities from competing. Against global warming. Prevent restrictive regulation on mandatory maintenance of electricity grid.

15. **Retail** $9,411,822

    Fight against raises in the minimum wage. Allow sourcing from China and other dictatorships. Reduce employee health insurance demands. Substitute temp workers for full-time workers. Minimize exposure to race-, gender-, and age-based discrimination lawsuits. Against unionization of workers.

16. Health $9,253,686

Maintain HMOs' liability protection from lawsuits, allow hospitals to differentially price and charge privately insured patients more than government-sponsored patients, and restrict malpractice awards against doctors. Against universal health care.

17. Gambling $8,446,200

Allow states to legalize gambling even though studies show for every $1 of state gambling tax revenue, the states absorb $3 of extra enforcement, health care, and other costs. Lobby for Internet gambling. Maintain Indian treaties with regard to gambling revenues.

18. Aerospace & Defense $8,147,652

Our biggest export is weapons. Always pushing for defense dollars to go toward new weapons systems rather than the troops.

19. Miscellaneous Business $8,047,228

Too many to list.

20. Food & Grocery Stores $7,479,587

Is it monopolistic that all cereal costs $3 a box when it can't cost $0.20 a box to make? Is it monopolistic when Coke pushes its competitors off the shelves by introducing so many varieties of its products? Are there unseen payoffs between food companies and grocers to ensure good product placement on store shelves? Against unionization and worker rights and benefits.

21. Engineering & Construction $5,478,131

In favor of big government projects, regardless of cost or benefit.

22. Tobacco $5,374,415

Prevent the FDA from regulating a product that is addictive to its customers and deadly. Avoid any future liability by restricting court judgments and writing new legislation restricting product liability.

23. Beer, Wine, & Liquor $5,348,153

Make sure no more prohibition. Avoid limitations on liquor advertising. Avoid advertising restrictions with new malt beverages.

24. Metals & Mining $5,265,193

Ease regulations against strip mining and pollution of water sources.

25. Agribusiness $4,649,700

Prevent regulation of genetically altered food. Maintain billions of dollars in government subsidies for ethanol, dairy, and sugar lobby. Maintain hundreds of billions of dollars of price supports for big agriculture in general.

26. Chemicals $4,537,949

Fight tougher environmental rules. Restrict liability due to plant site accidents. Restrict worker injury claims.

27. Accounting & Consulting $4,472,344

Trying to limit liability in Enron-type cases. Generate huge government consulting contracts. Avoid liability in client bankruptcies.

28. Automotive $4,428,586

Wants to end all discussion of mass transit as alternative to automobile. Doesn't want mpg standards applied to SUVs. Doesn't want to be forced to reduce pollution with alternative energy vehicles.

29. Tourism & Lodging $4,208,218

Avoid regulation and prosecution of corrupt charter vacation packages. Prevent restrictions on telemarketing.

30. Forest & Paper Products $3,520,878

Timber companies receive huge subsidy from government in use of public roads for logging and logging on public lands. Paper companies want air quality restrictions relaxed.

31. Restaurants $1,680,765

Allow paying restaurant workers below minimum wage so that tips make up difference. In favor of illegal immigration for staffing needs.

32. Machinery $1,612,950

Favor accelerated depreciation tax rules for companies buying new equipment.

33. International Trade $1,388,200

Want restrictions on trade reduced, at least trade from here to there. May support restrictions on agriculture, textiles, apparel, and footwear into this country to protect jobs and markets.

34. Textiles $1,194,755

In favor of severe tariff restrictions on foreign-made textiles.

35. Environmental & Waste Services $1,115,277

Waste service industry wants no regulation or investigation.

TOTAL $400,427,263

Source: For dollar amounts, www.commoncause.org. For narrative, the author.

You can see from the table that the securities and investments industry is the largest contributor. In addition to being very profitable, the securities business often acts as the leader of the entire business community because it has the rest of corporate America as investment banking clients and acts as their financier. Its products are corporate bonds and stocks that, by definition, do better when corporate America is doing better. As the profits and the market values of firms rise because of industry-favorable legislation coming out of Washington, the values of their securities rise—stocks, because earnings are improving, and bonds, because they are now less risky with greater equity cushion below them. This is good for the securities industry's own trading desk inventory of these instruments and their in-house arbitrage investment positions as well as for their investing clients' portfolios.

The second biggest listed contributor, though not an industry, is all labor unions. When it comes to making campaign contributions, labor unions are outspent about 11 to 1 by the total contributions of all industry (http://commoncause.org). The $32 million contributed by labor unions is a considerable sum, so labor unions are discussed in Chapter 6, where the effect of other noncorporate special interests is raised.

Other industries also benefit. Why else would the tobacco, gambling, and liquor industries be so generous with their giving? What kind of strange culture is it in which an addictive and deadly product like tobacco is legal and not acknowledged as a drug? How bizarre does the situation have to get before the American people say that enough is enough? The tobacco lobby may argue that prohibition of products rarely works, but there is no way tobacco should escape the scrutiny of the Federal Drug Administration (FDA); it clearly is a drug.

All currently successfully operating businesses share one attribute: They are incumbents, and as such, they all fear future competitors that might eventually strain their profit margins or bankrupt them. Therefore, it is in the interest of all well-established businesses to lobby our government to reinforce the status quo. One would expect them to be against innovation, against small business formation, and most definitely against allowing companies like themselves to fail through bankruptcy. They would naturally be in favor of whatever government support they could garner to avoid having to claim bankruptcy. But the continued existence of money-losing firms not only drains public funds that go to their life support, it also ties up valuable people and physical resources that might be better utilized in a different industry or business. When people are laid off, it can be good for an economy if they end up going from a declining industry into jobs in a more vibrant industry. Likewise, when firms go bankrupt, capital and human resources move out of slow to no growth companies and industries, and weak managements and inefficient operations eliminated.

There is no hard academic evidence to date that shows bankruptcies are bad for an economy (Richard Roll of the Anderson School 2003). But companies approaching bankruptcy ask Congress to save them, saying they are concerned not with themselves, but only with their employees, even if the management team in question hasn't thought of its employees once in the last decade without thinking about how it might take them for another nickel of pay. Society would be much better off if it allowed these poorly run firms to fail. Many of their employees will do fine finding new jobs, and if it is unconstrained by corporate lobbying, the government can be more generous with unemployment insurance plans so that the displaced who are unsuccessful in job placement immediately do not suffer harshly.

Allowing bankruptcies also serves notice to the rest of corporate America that the game is being played fairly and by the rules. If you do stupid things and take stupid risks in your business, you will not have the American taxpayer around to bail you out. This is an incredibly important concept to an economy because businesses must understand there are repercussions to taking bigger and bigger risks. Without the implied threat of bankruptcy, managements would naturally be steered toward riskier projects that probably would not match the risk profile of the companies' shareholders.

On December 11, 2003, the Supreme Court of the United States affirmed in a five-to-four vote the constitutionality of a new campaign finance law recently passed by Congress. The bill intended to eliminate "soft money" donations to national political parties, to put restrictions on the timing of when soft-money–funded organizations can run campaign advertisements, and to raise the limits on "hard money" donations to candidates to $2,000 per donor (*The New York Times,* 12/11/03).

While this is certainly a step in the right direction, many have already begun to express reservations as to the effectiveness of this new legislation. Senator Mitch McConnell, Republican of Kentucky, the chief critic of the new law in Congress, said that money will always find a way into the system. "This law will not remove one dime from politics," he said. Referring to the fact that soft money contributions will now go to third-party organizations rather than the national political parties, McConnell said, "Soft money is not gone; it has just changed its address" (*The New York Times,* 12/11/03).

Campaign experts say that money previously spent on television ads will now be directed to other forms of influence not regulated by the new law such as new issue-oriented lobbyists, direct mail, phone banks, and Internet sites. Wayne LaPierre, the executive vice president of the National Rifle Association (NRA), said his organization will just redirect the $25 million it spent on television ads in the 2002 elections. "We are going to be heard, I promise that. We have new lines on the football field, but the game is still going to be played" (*The New York Times,* 12/11/03).

So as a first step to try to get corporations out of the campaign contribution business, this is good news. Unfortunately, it looks as if moneyed interests will find ways to circumvent the law. Bush is expected to raise over $200 million in hard money contributions for the 2004 campaign and new third-party issue-oriented organizations have begun massive fundraising campaigns. There is no restriction in the law on corporations lobbying our government, and it appears they will find new avenues to get money to the candidates of their choice. Therefore, without any grounds well for publicly financed campaigns, it appears that in Washington it will be business as usual.

With corporations allowed to attack the societal and political fabric of America with their greedy campaign donations and lobbying, all Americans will be worse off. There will be some or all of the following:

- Less entrepreneurial activity

- Less new business formation

- Less new job growth

- Less government oversight

- More corruption

- Less transparency

- More emphasis on the status quo and less on innovation

- A great deal of resources wasted on old industries and old ideas

- Less voice for workers and citizens

This lobbying represents not only an unfair attempt to redistribute the country's precious resources but also a direct attack on America's democracy and our economy. It is an attack on our system of fairness and justice, the things an economy needs to encourage investment, the lifeblood of profitability, and growth. If people lose confidence in their government's ability to make the rules of the game fair and applicable to all, they will vote with their feet (La Porta et al., 1998). Personal savings will decline and personal investment will decline. People will spend less time on their own educational investment. Over time, the rich would get richer and the poor would have trouble keeping up. This is exactly what has been happening in America for the last 25 years.

Corporations lobbied for open U.S. borders and legal and illegal immigration into the U.S., especially of unskilled workers, mushroomed. The same corporations lobbied for global trade and now American workers are in competition with poorly organized workers the world over. As a result, U.S. workers' wages stagnated while executives' compensation packages soared. Unions became less important, union membership declined, and union wages, benefits, and work rules suffered. It became more difficult for minimum wage laws to keep up with inflation. Weapons, tobacco, and liquor became major exports for America. More and more industries were finding comfort in monopolistic or local monopoly pricing positions.

There is not a great deal of time to act to address the problem of excessive corporate lobbying and corporations' unjust campaign contributions. Very soon it will get to the point where any dissent along these lines either goes unheard or will be reported as un-American. The future, unfortunately, may already be here. Nothing is as un-American as what big corporations are doing to the American people and their freedom by the undue and unwanted influence of big business on our democratic government.

5

HOW THE RICH AND POWERFUL PLAY THE GAME

Many wealthy individuals in the U.S. play a game similar to the one played by America's biggest corporations in contributing heavily to political campaigns in exchange for favorable policy decisions. I am not interested in making a broad attack on the rich or in questioning their morality. I only wish to examine the effect on the society of having a wealthy class that has such enormous influence on the government. I am also not interested in starting a class war, which is often the charge raised whenever this issue surfaces. The class war, most likely, has already been started by the wealthy with their unusual and self-serving requests from our government, and it is the poor and middle classes who are experiencing the most battlefield casualties to date in the conflict.

The Christian Science Monitor reports that accusing people of dealing in "class warfare" has become very common in Washington. Criticizing CEO pay or discussing the possibility of increasing taxes on the wealthy immediately raises cries of class warfare. The Bush administration also has repeatedly gone to the class warfare argument, the paper reports. When people criticized Bush's plan to eliminate the tax on stock dividends because its benefits fell mostly to the rich, Bush said his critics were trying to "turn this into class warfare. That's not how I think." (*The Christian Science Monitor,* 9/23/03)

The past few decades have been very good for the wealthiest in the country. In 1980, the average CEO earned 42 times the average worker's salary. In 2001, that ratio had grown to 411 (*The Christian Science Monitor,* 9/23/03). In 2003, the average CEO pay at the 200 largest U.S. companies was $11.3 million (*Bloomberg News,* 12/30/03). A free marketer might argue that companies should be allowed to pay their CEOs whatever they wish, but proponents of this sentiment must also recognize that executive compensation committees of boards are often stacked with friends of the CEO. If boards did a better job of independently representing the interests of shareholders, they should have the right to set executive pay without interference from regulators.

At first blush, it might appear wise to allow your richest citizens to have greater input into the government because they typically are well educated and often have excellent business backgrounds. Wouldn't they know best which government policies would create the most productive of economies and most stable of regimes? Aren't they most qualified to manage the government? Again, once the facts are examined, it will be seen that the self-interest of the rich does not always align perfectly with the broader population; therefore, the wealthiest citizens may not be well representative of the populace in its entirety. And in pursuit of their narrow self-interests the wealthy, if given the chance, have an opportunity to destroy our economy and our democracy.

First a trick question—What do the leaders of all the countries of the world, all the Fortune 500 CEO's, almost every single U.S. Senator (*Wall Street Journal*, 06/25/02), and nearly all U.S. Ambassadors in the world have in common with the great majority of major individual donors to America's political candidates?

Yes, that's right—they are all rich! Americans are ruled both at work and in Washington by wealthy people. Wealth alone does not disqualify them from leadership; those who earned their wealth honestly through hard work do have some skills that were responsible for their wealth creation that might prove useful in leading the country and the economy. Washington insiders and the individual campaign contributors who try to influence them all share this attribute of being somewhat wealthy. Therefore, you would expect them to see eye to eye on matters that affect rich people and their wealth, even if the policies they advocate harm average Americans.

Why didn't the Democratic party object more strenuously to Bush's income, dividend and inheritance tax cuts, whose benefits accrued almost exclusively to the wealthy? The reason is that most of the Democratic party heavyweights, insiders, major contributors, and lobbyists are themselves quite wealthy. The Democratic party needs to go back to their roots and start representing the common people again. Unfortunately, if they did so, the Democrats would lose many of their biggest and wealthiest contributors.

The problem with wealthy people having a supernormal influence on the government is not just that it is unfair and usurps the principle of one person/one vote. This alone is, of course, reason enough to curtail their campaign contribution practices. But more important, a society that does not ensure fairness in setting the rules of behavior plants the seed of its own undoing. Such a system is a direct attack on the democratic institutions Americans hold dear, remembering their importance to a well-functioning society and a vibrant economy. Societies collapse when participants lose confidence and trust that the system will be fair and just to all.

Eventually, if the systemic problems are ignored, they can lead to a direct attack on the democracy itself. The warning signs are everywhere. Only 50% of eligible voters typically vote in an American presidential election (http://commoncause.org). What do you think those other 50% are saying? Democracies begin to perish when a majority of citizens no longer think it important to vote. (It is hard to differentiate by voting turnout numbers alone a truly apathetic electorate from one that is intentionally withdrawing its support of the regime because it recognizes that government by the people has been modified to mean government by the wealthiest people.)

We have argued that corporations, by law, have one objective: maximizing their shareholders' wealth. This prevents them from taking a wider social perspective, and thus they should not be allowed to lobby or contribute to the government.

Although wealthy individuals, unlike corporations, are not obliged by legal precedent to consider only their own wealth maximization, their frequently observed self-centered actions might make it appear that they are. Economic theory predicts that wealthy people would have much less use for their last dollar of earnings than poorer people would because most of their needs would have already been satisfied and they would have an additional reserve of unspent dollars in the bank for insurance purposes. Unfortunately, many rich people seem to crave every marginal additional dollar of income, and this craving seems to increase, not decrease, as they get wealthier. This phenomenon has never been adequately explained in the economic, or psychiatric, literature, but it appears to be more complicated than simply expanding the same self-seeking behavior that contributed to making them wealthy to begin with. Should the most self-centered and richest people in our country be given the responsibility to run the government which has the unenviable task of trying to provide care for the nation's most unfortunate?

Wall Street tells a story about the insatiable greed of the wealthy. Mike Milken and Fred Joseph of Drexel Burnham were arguing over Milken's year-end personal bonus for 1987. The meeting should have been a formality because Milken's bonus was determined arithmetically as a percentage of total junk bond revenues at the firm. By formula that year, it was to be $780 million for Milken personally, based on the amount of junk bond business his group in Los Angeles had transacted. The meeting, however, was rumored to be a three-hour screaming match because the two could not decide whether an additional bonus of $55,000 was also due Milken for a previously overlooked junk bond transaction.

What do wealthy campaign contributors have in common that might bias their view or make it significantly different from that of the general population? First, most of them, or their ancestors, have been incredibly successful in business. Typically, that is where most of their wealth originated. They therefore will naturally have a positive view of business and possibly, but not necessarily, less experience in other forms of human endeavor such as the arts, literature, academia, or government. This gives their life perspective a business focus and reinforces that of the corporate lobbyists who already have enormous government influence. Many wealthy people are libertarians because they like the idea of few taxes, no government interference in business and a world in which dollar votes decide most everything. The philosophical problem with the libertarian movement is that it is hard to find a poor libertarian. It is a philosophy that appeals mostly to the haves and not the have-nots.

Second, and more important, they are all investors because that's what rich people do with their cash—they invest it. In addition, many own their own businesses. It's not that they do not work hard; it is just that when they become wealthy, their investment earnings come to dominate their salaried earnings.

People are always curious to know whether they themselves qualify as rich. Here is a simple hypothetical test to see whether you are a worker bee or a queen bee, recognizing that the line of demarcation is wholly arbitrary. Answer this question honestly: Would you rather have a permanent annual salary increase of, say, 20% or have your total savings increase 20%? If you opted for the salary increase, you can keep buzzing—you're a worker bee! This contrasts greatly with the government's view, which is that most Americans are now considered investors because the 401(k) participation rate is 72.6% among workers (*Wall Street Journal,* 11/19/03). *USA Today* (11/17/03) reports that most of these 401(k) accounts are quite small, over 42% of workers are cashing out their 401(k) accounts when they change jobs, and only 30% of Americans are looking to their investments to help them with their retirement. Unfortunately, if you aren't idle, you probably are not part of the idle rich.

The reason that it is important to realize that all campaign contributors think like investors is that investors do not necessarily think like the rest of us. Investors want to see companies' stocks increase, which means they want earnings to increase. That means they are in favor of keeping wages low. Generally, they would be in favor of longer work weeks, less overtime, no minimum wage, fewer benefits, smaller pensions, no health care benefits, and no paid maternal leaves. One can see that the wishes of the wealthy campaign contributors do not match well with the wishes of average working Americans.

With regard to growth, the wealthy would be all for it, at almost any social cost (Greider, 1997). The reason is simple: Their stock portfolios will appreciate in value much faster overriding any ill effects that the uncontrolled growth might cause in their lives. Given their wealth, they are also in a position to shield themselves from most of the ill effects the society or the environment might suffer from such growth. Wealthy people don't drive in congested traffic; the poorer ones sit in the back of limousines and the richer ones fly in their helicopters. Who cares about dirty rivers? Only poor people drink tap water. And how does one escape the poor air quality in Los Angeles? You live in Malibu on the ocean in the summer and vacation in Aspen in the mountains in the winter—the air is fine there.

If you are rich and concerned about your stock portfolio, why would you ever oppose the defense establishment, tobacco companies, or weapons manufacturers? You own all their stocks. Your broker calls it being properly diversified. When you hear on the news that Ford Explorers are turning over and killing their occupants, you feel a touch of sadness, but then you remember you unloaded your Ford stock last month, so you get over it. Can you see how the wealthy might be against consumer protection activities and try to limit corporate liability for companies' products?

So the wealthy, because of their investor mindset, have motivations and aspirations far different from those of the average American. At least many of them own their own businesses, so one can expect them to be more sympathetic than big corporations to the regulatory and other burdens of small business owners. But the bottom line is that the rich are not like you and me.

The most important political and economic issue for the wealthy is and always has been taxes! As discussed earlier, that last dollar of earnings is awfully important to them, and it is not easy to get it away from them. They dislike all taxes, but they especially detest those that hit the wealthy disproportionately. So, as you might expect, they are in favor of flat income tax rates and against progressive rates. It doesn't make much sense to have a self-interested wealthy segment of the population decide how progressive our tax system should be without the input of average Americans whose pocketbooks will be dramatically impacted. Regressive taxes such as the Social Security payroll tax and state sales taxes have increased recently while there have been reductions in progressive taxes such as the capital gains tax, the dividends tax, the top income tax rate, and the inheritance tax. This is clear evidence that the wealthy are benefiting monetarily from their cozy relationship with our elected representatives.

In 2001, the Bush administration passed an income tax cut that saw 42% of the benefits accrue to the richest 1% of Americans as measured by income. Families with annual incomes over $1 million, a mere 0.13% of the population, will receive 17.3% of the proceeds from the tax cut. In 2003, Bush again cut taxes. In selling his plan, administration spokespeople used the catch phrase, "92 million Americans will receive an average tax cut of $1,083." While this is technically true, the administration used statistical tricks to inflate people's perception of how big a tax cut they might receive. Fifty million taxpayers received no tax cut at all, and about half of all American families received a tax cut of less than $100 (*The New York Times*, 9/14/03). Some argue that the rich should get most of the tax cuts because the wealthy pay most of the taxes. But this ignores that the rich also make most of the money in the country and rebating taxes to them is a poor way to jump start a depressed economy.

Recently, the wealthy have campaigned to try to have the estate or inheritance tax eliminated. Inheritance taxes are levied on couples with estates valued over $1.3 million (Internal Revenue Service), which means only very rich people are taxed. In lobbying for the estate tax cut, the administration tried to give the impression that many small farms and small businesses would benefit from the tax reduction. But because of the large exemption, only 2% of estates end up paying any inheritance tax at all, and most of the taxes raised are paid by a few thousand estates (Krugman, 2003). The most egregious fact is that the very, very wealthy pay no inheritance tax as they utilize tax avoidance schemes to forego any tax liability.

That does not mean that only rich people are affected by the elimination of the inheritance tax, however. If there were no inheritance tax, a great deal of unusual privilege and economic power could be passed from one generation to the next. A basic tenet of the society is that there should be equal opportunity for all. How can this be accomplished when a baby born in the ghetto comes into the world with nothing and a wealthy family's baby is born primed to inherit a fortune? What kind of equal opportunity is there when a wealthy child has all the advantages of class, including better early nourishment, better neighborhoods, better schools, and better connected friends?

The world is inherently unfair, but some things, like the inheritance tax, can make the playing field a bit more level and give everyone a fair chance at success. Natively brilliant people will have an advantage in life, and there is little that can be done about this other than to encourage everyone to study hard. But the unfair access to opportunities that comes with inherited wealth is easily solved by an inheritance tax, and rescinding it is a move in the wrong direction. In addition, if the inheritance tax is revoked, the contribution those taxes make to pay for the cost of governing still has to come from somewhere. If the wealthy are deciding, it will most likely come from increased regressive taxes or reduced government benefits for everyone else.

Of course, the wealthy are always in favor of a capital gains tax cut. They have over $10 trillion tied up in low-basis assets that they would love to sell without paying taxes. They don't need a permanent reduction—just one day of tax relief to sell their low-basis assets. And, oh, what a day it would be!

So as the rich have voted themselves lower and lower taxes (*Newsweek*, 12/1/03), what has happened to the middle class? Many are paying higher income taxes because of the Alternative Minimum Tax (*USA Today*, 12/2/03). They are also paying more property taxes, higher state and local taxes, especially sales taxes, and ever-increasing payroll taxes to fund Social Security. The rich have gotten their wish; they have made overall taxes much more regressive. Do you think a fair tax system should minimize or contribute to the dramatic difference in incomes between the wealthiest and the poorest in the country?

Because one group of wealthy citizens has too much political power, it seems to be violating all sense of fairness. But there is much greater damage being done. In the most recent tax-cut debate, the well-connected wealthy showed an incredible ability to cut off their nose to spite their face. They seemed honestly excited about a tax cut for themselves, even if it meant damaging the growth of the overall economy. The tax cuts of 2001 and 2003 would grant a $3.8 trillion giveaway to the wealthiest, would obliterate a $2 billion surplus and create total government deficits of approximately $1.8 trillion over the next 10 years (*The New York Times*, 3/26/03). (Please remember, $1 trillion is the same magnitude as a million bags of money, each containing $1 million.) And because most of the tax cuts will go to the wealthy, the money will end up in bank accounts with little real long-term stimulus to the economy. Christmas spending in 2003 was pretty much flat with the exception of high end luxury retailers who were soaking in the wealthy's tax cut rebates. If anything was learned from the Clinton administration, it was that investors in an economy prefer a government that can manage its own finances without having to resort to excessive borrowing or inflating its currency to fund deficits. But these wealthy folks seem to be taking a bird in the hand in the form of an immediate tax cut rather than the possible strong growth in their portfolios from a future strong economy.

Supply-side economists argue that tax cuts are the key to stimulating growth, but they have been unable to demonstrate this in any empirical research study. Getting money away from a wasteful government might be good, but giving it to the wealthy makes little sense as a stimulatory action. It turns out that in terms of tax rates, the very wealthy in the country are paying at a lower and lower rate each year.

There are other important differences between rich folk and poor and middle-class folks. Even though many rich people have children, they can afford to be much more hawkish in solving the country's international disputes. The reason is simple: Rich kids typically don't go to war. They don't go now because the pay is terrible given the risk, and they didn't go when there was a draft because many of them got deferments, arranged by their politically connected parents. If poor and middle-class American families end up offering their sons and daughters to fight in American wars, they alone should decide when, and if, America fights its next war.

The wealthy also are for the status quo. They should be in favor of growth opportunities in their community, but if growth threatens their leadership position in the community, they would rather pass. Old money is very conservative, averse to change, and supportive of tradition and culture. In other words, the rich get to keep their positions of prestige and power. They will vote to maintain the status quo. Why would they want any change that might threaten their incumbency?

This emphasis on maintaining the status quo can be extremely damaging to the operation of a healthy economy. Such powerful incumbents can have a devastating effect on new company formation and new wealth creation. At its most cynical, such a philosophy is against ensuring the general education of the public or providing economic opportunities to the masses because such good works may just create the next economic competitor for the established wealthy class.

The wealthy elite will do whatever it can to preserve its political power. While campaign financing turns slowly into an extortion game with both parties hitting up the same major contributors, the wealthy will continue to play, if only to preserve their political status. They will fight initiatives that might dilute their political power, like the recent motor-voter initiative that would have made voter registration easier by allowing people to register to vote at the same time they register their cars. And they will fight to the death against meaningful campaign finance reform.

This corruption of America's democracy by the wealthy runs deep. It is not just in the federal government. It resides in state legislatures, governors' offices, city councils, school boards, and zoning committees. Serious campaign money has begun to infiltrate the state office races. Millions of dollars are being spent by the wealthy in California to influence minor political races such as the makeup of the school board in San Diego (*San Diego Tribune,* 11/8/2000). Even if money is not changing hands aboveboard, you can be sure the wealthy have their causes represented. Take a look at the membership of most cities' zoning boards. Do these people truly look independent to you? Why do they always seem to vote for greater and greater development at the cost of increased congestion and pollution? Typically, these zoning boards are controlled by the real estate developers and pro-growth business people in town who have the most to gain from development.

Although a healthy society should not act out of jealousy or envy in attacking the richer classes' rights to property, it also has a responsibility to ensure that the wealthy are not misusing their economic power to unfairly prejudice the government. The rich can buy as many yachts as they want, but the purchase of just one legislator is one too many. Corporations need to see that it is in their interest to create healthy new markets for their goods around the world by beginning to promote the stability inherent in democracy. By the same token, the wealthy here at home must realize that greater involvement by the common people in their government will result in a stronger, more broad-based economy and greater prosperity for all, including greater growth in their own rather substantial investment portfolios.

6

OTHER SPECIAL INTERESTS HAVE OTHER SPECIAL REQUESTS

Corporations and wealthy individuals account for the majority of the dollar contributions to America's elected representatives, but Table 6.1 shows that many other special-interest groups spend a great deal of their time lobbying the government to gain special advantages. This is a very small sample of all the lobbying efforts in Washington. The entire list could fill a phone book ... and it does: the Washington, D.C. phone book.

Lobbying organizations represent powerful political groups. Because each concentrates its firepower on one particular set of issues, these organizations can have a great influence on the way laws are written and policy is conducted. And for this reason, even though, unlike corporations, they may represent real U.S. citizens, special-interest lobbies can still damage the political process by elevating their clients' self-interest over that of the public, especially with regard to the narrow legislative focus they practice.

Table 6.1 Our Country's Problems and the Special Interest Groups
Chosen to Solve Them

PROBLEM	PROBLEM SOLVER
Failure of public schools	Teachers and administrators
Election laws	Incumbents
Corporate corruption	Accounting firms
Military spending	Defense contractors
Global warming	Coal-fired utilities
Drug costs	Pharmaceutical companies
Social security	AARP
Complex tax code	IRS
Zoning laws and congestion	Real estate developers
Tobacco restrictions	Tobacco company law firms
Israel/Palestinian conflict	Jewish lobby
Gas mileage and auto pollution	Auto manufacturers
Justice system	Lawyers
Wages and benefits	Unions
Legalized gambling	Casinos
Inefficient government	Government employees

Through their lobbyists, special interests enjoy the same kind of disproportionate representation that was discussed earlier concerning campaign contributions. One party should not be able to increase its political power on any issue beyond one person/one vote, whether by trying to buy additional influence or by concentrating its lobbying efforts on one issue. Both are niche strategies that are effective in the economic marketplace but extremely harmful in the marketplace of public goods that is the government. At least many special interest groups have some American citizens' interests at heart, something that cannot be said about the corporate lobby.

Forty years ago, Washington was a fairly small city. Now it is teeming with lobbyists; K Street is dedicated to them, and the surrounding metropolitan area is full of new buildings to house them. Washington is seeing extraordinary growth as the population in the greater metropolitan area including Baltimore and Northern Virginia is now approaching eight million people (U.S. Census 2000 PHC-T-3. Ranking Tables for Metropolitan Areas: 2000— www.census.gov). Rush hour is unbearable and urban sprawl is so bad that the beautiful forested countryside of Northern Virginia has become one vast strip mall. And this in a city that has no discernable major industry other than lobbyists pressing favors from the government.

These lobbying organizations have acted as logjams in some of the country's most pressing problems over time. The solution to any difficult political problem typically involves some give and take on all sides. Examining Table 6.1 in greater detail, one can see that while the special interest group named is not always the source of the problem, its insistence that its or its clients' interests not be harmed often stands in the way of constructive solutions to the problems listed. For example, incumbent politicians would be hesitant to rewrite campaign laws that might give challengers a better chance of unseating an incumbent. The AARP (formerly the American Association of Retired Persons) will go out of its way to protect Social Security for current retirees but is less concerned with the tax burden this places on future generations or their probability of ever receiving similar retirement benefits. And automobile manufacturers will promote the cleanliness of their cars as long as they are allowed by Congress to continue to exempt their SUVs from automobile gas mileage standards.

To demonstrate that many political problems, including those listed in Table 6.1, have ready and reasonable solutions that would appeal to most Americans and to convince you that the major stumbling block to adopting these solutions is the special-interest lobbying force supposedly dedicated to solving the problem, the following sections discuss political solutions that have the general public's interests at heart. The suggested solutions all share common attributes: namely, all parties are harmed a little bit, but through cooperative effort and smart government action, all reach a nice consensus solution that makes the country and the people better off. Of course, each of the major lobbying parties identified in Table 6.1 must also share some of the pain, but not unduly so.

The first example of a festering problem with no practical solution proposed by the government is the quality of the public elementary and secondary schools. Our children's future depends on rectifying this problem as does the future of America because education has long been believed to be closely tied to economic progress (Solow, 1956 and Barro, 1991). The teachers' union and the school administrators represent one special interest and are now in a battle with corporate America, acting in its own self-interest, about whether to privatize our public schools. Unfortunately, parents who seem to know what is best for their children have not organized their own effective lobbying force in Washington and so are excluded from the current debate.

Education is typically a local issue with problems resolved at the community and state levels. That has changed with Washington now taking a more activist role. The Senate Appropriations Committee and the full House of Representatives took advantage of Washington D.C.'s unique status of receiving its school funding directly from the federal government to approve a private school voucher measure in 2003 as part of broader bills appropriating funds for the city. The bill would provide vouchers worth up to $7,500 a year to low-income Washington D.C. families with children in poorly performing schools. The total cost of the initial program is $13 million. The vouchers could be used at private schools, including religious ones. (*Education Week,* 9/24/03).

A number of major cities, including New York City, have also begun pilot programs with the Edison Project, founded by Chris Whittle, to privatize some of their public schools. (Whittle also founded Channel One, which provides television programming and advertising to over 12,000 elementary and secondary schools; see www.edisonproject.com.) Such a corporate privatization of the schools might lead to enormous efficiency gains, and if market competition is introduced, privatized schooling may lead to a more affordable education for our children. Given corporate America's track record, however, it may not be advisable to entrust this group with the education of our youth. As part of their education, school-children might be initiated into a corporate world of marketing, advertising, brand names, promotion, and encouraged dumbed-down consumption. Would corporate America put much value in teaching our children the classics in literature, music theory, foreign languages, economic history, or any of the fine arts? It might be better if teachers not have a preconceived, corporate-approved agenda when it comes to teaching our children.

One potential solution to this dilemma is to allow vouchers at schools but have them accepted only in public schools. Because public schools are free, a public school voucher, at least initially, would not have a monetary value but rather act as a coupon redeemable at any public school for one year of education for a child. Students who worked harder and got better grades might get a priority voucher that allowed them access to the most desired schools.

Some of the better public schools would have an excess of students wanting to attend and "spend" their vouchers there, resulting in their eventual expansion and pay increases for the teachers and administrators. Failing schools would have a dearth of vouchers submitted by students, resulting in wage reductions, job layoffs, and eventual closure if the problems were not corrected. Obviously, not all students would be able to attend the best school, but at least this modified voucher plan would put pressure on the worst-performing schools to either improve or face closure. New administrations and new faculties could replace failing staffs at the bankrupted schools if entirely new schools could not be afforded.

Why hasn't such a purely public school voucher proposal even been suggested in Washington? From a special-interest perspective, it is the worst kind of initiative. It upsets the interests of not one, but four very powerful special interests in Washington. First, corporations don't benefit; they are excluded from the party because corporate privatization of the schools would no longer be necessary. Second, most wealthy persons don't benefit because many already have their kids in private schools and wouldn't be getting any vouchers as they would under the private school voucher plan. Third, the teachers union and the school administrators would never let the program happen because it threatens their job stability. Fourth, the religious right has always viewed private voucher plans as a way for the government to partially fund the cost of private religious schools. The only beneficiaries would be the American people and our children, and unfortunately, the way America's government is organized today, that is a truly silent and underserved majority.

Another major problem facing America today is that the Social Security system, by almost anyone's estimate, is due to explode in the not-too-distant future. This is a fascinating problem to discuss because most Americans believe that it is an intractable problem, as certain to occur as the sun rising in the East. When the problem is presented, it is usually done with a great deal of reliance on numbers, demographic statistics, and actuarial tables, so it makes it very difficult to clearly understand the basic issues involved. No matter how you analyze it, the problem is so big that there is no possible solution. When baby boomers start retiring in approximately six years, there will never be enough active workers to fund the entire payments required by retirees. The only provisional solution offered is for workers to retire at 75 rather than 65, which is a plan not overly offensive to authors, but extremely so to roofers.

Larry Kotlikoff (2001) of Boston University described the magnitude of the problem, and this was before the 2003 Bush tax cut. He said the Social Security and Medicare programs are underfunded by some 40%. To close this gap, the combined employee/employer payroll tax will have to increase by 67%. Even more startling, to fairly tax the baby boomer generation who garner most of the retirement benefits of Social Security and currently low taxes, income taxes should be raised by 68% immediately, which is just the opposite of what Bush accomplished by his tax cut in 2003. Kotlikoff says that 77 million baby boomers are going to switch very soon from changing diapers to wearing them, and he wonders how 15% more workers will pay the benefits of 100% additional retirees. Those over 85, the group most likely to have expensive chronic care needs, will grow from 3 million today to over 28 million in 2050 (American Association of Homes and Services for the Aging at www.aahsa.org).

The government is not fully disclosing the magnitude of this problem. The Social Security Technical Panel on Assumptions and Methods concluded the government was understating the size of a potential underfunding in Social Security. It assumed too-low levels of immigration, did not allow for longer life expectancies and did not adjust for a world with lower inflation (MSNBC News at www.msnbc.com, 10/23/03). Because the Social Security system is currently running a temporary surplus with the large number of baby boomers working, the government is also understating the true government deficit due to its general operations. For the 2004 fiscal year, this on-budget deficit without including the Social Security surplus is expected to be $639 billion, not the $455 billion the administration estimated after taking advantage of the Social Security surplus (*The New York Times,* 1/23/03).

What is most frustrating about the Social Security problem is the inherent unfairness of it. Because Social Security is a pay-as-you-go system, the post–baby boomers who pay in throughout their whole working lives will not be able to attain an adequate retirement income but will have to face much higher tax rates. That is just math. The reason the problem seems unsolvable is that one normally assumes the same constraints that Congress does; that is, the solution cannot harm the most powerful special-interest group involved, the AARP, which represents those who are already collecting their Social Security checks or soon will be. It is true that if a condition of the problem is that no harm comes to some Americans who happen to be members of AARP, a reasonable solution is nearly impossible. But if the problem is not addressed, many, many more Americans will come to harm than necessary, and most will suffer real hardship upon retirement, and for a completely unjust reason.

This is why government is necessary. America's representatives should be forward thinking in order to plan ahead to avoid hardship and suffering for the country's citizens and to act fairly and justly in all its deliberations and actions. What might the government do today to avert this tragedy if it ignored the protestations of the AARP and focused on the welfare of all the country's citizens, the elderly of today and the elderly of tomorrow?

The solution is straightforward. The real hardship comes to this and future generations only if their Social Security income in retirement represents the major portion of their total income and accumulated wealth. Losing $1,000 to $1,500 a month is extremely painful to someone for whom it is the only source of income, but it is much less painful to someone who has many other sources of income and significant investments and assets. Economic theorists always assumed that retirees would save during their lifetime and then in retirement sell assets, disinvest, and consume. Retirees should not be able to avoid having to sell their accumulated assets in order to fund their retirement. In addition, some retirees are veterans of at least one of three major conflicts—World War II, Korea, or Vietnam—and are receiving a military pension. Finally, this generation worked during a time that saw strong unions and public and private pensions that have very generous benefits associated with them judged by today's standards.

Contrast this scenario with that for the next couple of generations. Very few post–baby boomers are wealthy, many younger people are new immigrants to the country holding lower-paying jobs, and corporate pensions have been restructured over the last 20 years to be much less generous in retirement. Many defined benefit pension plans have been replaced by defined contribution plans in which the retiree bears all the market risk.

So looking across generations and ignoring which particular generation you belong to, you'll see the key to avoiding real hardship on anyone's behalf is to make Social Security means tested. Those who need it to get by will get it, but there is no reason to pay it to the already wealthy. And the means test should take into account not just other incomes but also accumulated property, assets, and investments. In addition to saving the system right now and keeping the retirement age from rising to 80, making the system needs based would also allow today's workers to make dramatically lower payroll tax contributions. In trying to fund their own and previous generations' retirements, the present generation of workers is so overtaxed, especially the middle class and the working poor, that saving is almost impossible. No one would be able to opt out of the new system because there is no way to tell who might be in need in the future (W. Talbott, 2004), but the total required contribution would be much lower, reflecting the fact that it would now be a real insurance premium against retiring with little income as opposed to a handout to the rich.

Those who have paid in over time are going to say that the rules were changed. Well they were but for good reason. The old system was bankrupt and broken. The alternative would be to keep paying out benefits, overtax the young, and never provide them with any retirement benefits, and that doesn't make much sense. If there is insufficient moneys to provide a decent retirement income for the needy, any deficit could easily be filled in with a real inheritance tax. Remember, you can't take it with you.

The AARP surprisingly was a major proponent of the Medicare reform bill passed by the Bush administration in 2003, which will make it more difficult for many elderly citizens to afford appropriate medical care. With 35 million members, more than one-tenth of the American population, and hundreds of millions in annual income from the sale of insurance and other products to its members, the AARP is perhaps the wealthiest and most influential advocacy group in the country. Some democrats accused the AARP of supporting the legislation to help its insurance business, highlighting a problem if political advocacy groups also are involved in private enterprise. William D. Novelli, the CEO of the AARP since 2000, was criticized for not consulting with his membership on such an important piece of legislation (*The New York Times,* 11/26/03).

To the extent that the AARP speaks for only Americans over 50 years old, it may have serious conflicts of interest with its own private-sector businesses, and has potential agent/client conflict problems with its own membership does not bode well for America. Should this one organization have such unusual access to and influence with the government on issues affecting all Americans, even those under the age of 50?

What about the Israeli-Palestinian conflict? The conflict is enormously complex, and finding a solution is clearly outside the scope of this text, but does the Jewish-American lobby in the United States share some of the blame for there not being a resolution to the conflict to date? As of the middle of 2003, at least 2,100 Palestinians and 700 Israelis had been killed since the latest uprising began (*The Nation,* 5/19/03).

A poll conducted in late 2003 by Eurobarometer that contacted 7,500 people from the European Union (500 from each EU state), reported that a majority of those polled ranked Israel as the country that poses the greatest threat to world peace. Almost 60% of the Europeans surveyed believe Israel is more dangerous to world peace than North Korea, Iran, Iraq, and Afghanistan. The United States was ranked sixth most dangerous on the list (*El Pais,* Spain's leading newspaper, 10/30/03). Israel's Diaspora Affairs Minister Natan Sharansky accused Europeans of being anti-Semitic, and the Los Angeles-based Simon Wiesenthal Centre, which fights anti-Semitism, said that the EU should not have any further role in the Israeli/Palestinian peace talks as a result of this poll (*The Star,* 11/03/03).

Clearly, those Europeans polled see the conflict in Palestine quite differently than does the pro-Israel lobby in Washington. There is a likelihood that some of the Europeans' responses were clouded by anti-Semitism and prejudice, but there is also the very real possibility that the pro-Israeli lobby in Washington is unfairly influencing the United States government to take too strong of a pro-Israeli position in the conflict. If this is true, it makes America's role as unbiased peacemaker difficult because the Palestinians will be suspicious of our motives in any U.S.-negotiated peace plan.

When President Bush tried to insist that Israel take more moderate actions regarding the Palestinians, such as removing some of the settlements in the West Bank or announcing a formal recognition of a Palestinian state, 80 senators and 240 members of Congress signed a petition circulated by the pro-Israeli lobby insisting that the Palestinians take the first step (*The New York Times,* 4/17/03). Such demands as to who will act first ensure that a conflict such as this will go on ad infinitum. It seems reasonable that Israel insist on seeing some good faith on behalf of the Palestinians first by insisting terrorist acts cease, and yet that presumes that the Palestinian authority has control over such terrorist groups as Hamas and Hezbollah. Palestinians could just as easily argue that Israel should take the first step by removing some of the settlements. Maybe enacting a less-than-perfect compromise is in order, and it should be followed by a mutual crackdown on violence on both sides.

If America ignored the pro-Israeli lobbyists at home and pushed Israel to take a more moderate position with regard to the creation of a Palestinian state, the removal of the Israeli settlements in the West Bank and stopping construction of the wall in the West Bank, all Americans might feel more comfortable leading an international coalition to maintain the peace and prevent any terrorist acts against Israel. Israel, by its aggressive reaction to the Palestinian suicide bombers, prevents any broad support in the world to encourage and enforce a peace in the area. As America is finding out in Iraq, overreacting to terrorists plays right into their hands.

If the U.S. government strongly supported a more moderate and prudent peace plan in Palestine, America would be better off, the Palestinians would be better off, and surprisingly, so would Israel because peace might bring better economic times for its long-suffering people. Israelis themselves must face the daily threat of terrorism in their country as well as exploding budget deficits and unemployment north of 11%. A recent poll by Israel's Jaffee Institute for Strategic Studies shows that 56% of Israelis—up from 48 percent last year—would "support a unilateral withdrawal from the territories in the context of a peace accord, even if that meant ceding all settlements" (*The Nation,* 6/30/2003).

I don't want to suggest that the Palestinians are not without blame. They only hurt their own cause with their suicidal violence. Any Palestinians fighting to push Israel into the sea deserve a violent response from Israel. If they were smart, the Palestinians would adopt a Gandhi-inspired plan of nonviolent resistance and demand an ethical response from Israel and the world with regard to their demands for a homeland. The Israelis, of all people in the world, should understand a people striving to create their own homeland.

What about the drug war? If the police and prison guards were taken out of the lobbying business, wouldn't most Americans recognize that drug addiction is an illness and not a crime? Even if Americans were afraid to legalize drugs for fear that their use might expand, they could endorse treatment options rather than prison. It's easy to paint drug offenders as bad people because their need to support their habit can drive them to theft and violence. But by now, almost every American has a family member or close friend who has been debilitated by this illness. These loved ones are not criminals. President Bush knows this best of all. President Bush, his two daughters, and his niece have all had problems with alcohol and/or drug addiction. How he approves prison sentences for three-strike drug offenders of 20 years in prison with a clear conscious is beyond comprehension. If drug users were successfully treated medically rather than considered common criminals, the police and prison guard lobby might suffer as the number of prisoners shrank and the demand for new prisons evaporated, but wouldn't the rest of us, including the addicted, be much better off? The absence of a sure-fire proven medical therapy for curing alcoholism and drug addiction does not justify putting its victims in prison.

Nearly 1 out of every 150 people in America is in prison or jail; this is a figure no other democracy in the world comes close to matching. Many are there for drug offenses (60% of federal offenders and 22% of state and local inmates). Twenty-five percent of black Americans spend some time behind bars during their lives. The total number of Americans behind bars is currently over two million, and this number has tripled since 1980 (*The New York Times,* 3/7/99).

Four hundred thousand people are incarcerated for drug offenses and a third of these, simply for drug possession. Virtually alone among Western democracies, the United States has chosen a plan of incarceration to deal with drug offenders. General Barry McCaffrey, the nation's former drug czar, calls it "America's internal gulag" (*The New York Times,* 3/7/99).

The stock price of the Corrections Corporation of America, the nation's largest private prison company, has increased tenfold since 1994. To provide for the increase in the number of inmates, the U.S. is currently building one new prison per week, making it one of its best growth industries. Unions representing prison guards are the fastest-growing public employee associations in many states and are some of the strongest and most vocal lobbying forces (*The New York Times,* 3/7/99).

It is hard to get a good read on what the American people think about this issue because they have been bombarded with information from only one side. Illicit drugs will probably never be legalized in our lifetime because America has made too big a business out of criminalizing users. Prisons now are a multibillion-dollar industry that sucks the life out of our youngest citizens. But it is fair to say that the debate would be more intelligent and more inclusive if the police, prison guards, and prison operating companies did not have such a strong lobbying voice with our government.

One of the strongest lobbies in Washington is the military industrial complex. In addition to direct lobbying on behalf of military contractors, defense companies have funded a number of Washington-based think tanks that espouse an extremely hawkish world view, encourage greater defense spending, and spend a great deal of their time lobbying the government. In a world of exploding deficits and concern about wasteful government spending, why is the government spending $401 billion on defense in fiscal 2004? (not including another $59 billion estimated for Iraq and Afghanistan). Why are there still forces in Europe after the demise of the Soviet Union? What are American troops doing in South Korea other than making themselves a potential target for an attack from the north?

Bush is currently spending money on both guns and butter, making big defense expenditures around the world at the same time he is elevating domestic spending. This type of spending is not sustainable in the long term (*The New York Times,* 12/7/03). Most disturbing is that many of the military spending increases go to weapons systems procurements from those big defense contractors most expert at lobbying while American armed forces and their families get by on very low salaries and fairly inadequate housing.

The average American is very much antiwar and believes war should be used only as a last resort. The world has changed with the introduction of worldwide terrorism and suicide bombers. Do you really think a traditional military force will be effective in eliminating, or even reducing this threat? As America bombs the countries that supposedly support terrorism, do you think recruitment to terrorist organizations has increased or decreased? Do you think military force could prevent a single individual from committing terrorist acts anywhere in the world if all it takes is a bottle of gasoline purposely ignited in a Tokyo subway to claim 140 lives?

We have entered a brave new world with terrorism, and the logical first reaction is to try to outlaw it and prevent it, but this effort will fail miserably. Even the defense lobbyists slowed their lobbying efforts immediately after 9/11 for fear of appearing to exploit a tragedy (*Congressional Quarterly Weekly,* 10/13/01). There has to be a new approach to terrorism, one that will not needlessly continue to build America's conventional military forces or dramatically constrain our civil liberties. Without directly negotiating with terrorists, America will have to come to understand the concerns of young people around the world most influenced by their message and, where feasible, address them.

In this brave new world, there has been a fundamental power shift from large countries with traditional military might to smaller movements able to access more mobile weapons of mass destruction. If any good can come out of this power shift away from traditional military might, it may be that finally the concept that might is right will be exposed as morally bankrupt and future conflicts will have to be decided through negotiation and understanding rather than a show of military might.

These other special interests' power in Washington pales in comparison with the biggest lobbying force, the corporate lobbying effort. Of course, if the biggest lobbying force in Washington, the business and corporate lobby, were eliminated, problems in America would start to solve themselves. For example, let's examine the appropriate level of the minimum wage in this country. If McDonald's and other retail businesses got out of the lobbying business, don't you think most Americans would be in favor of a real minimum living wage sufficient for working parents to raise a family on? The restaurant lobby is a potent force that leads the fight to keep the minimum wage low (*Congress Daily,* 9/20/01), currently in real dollar terms below its level of 40 years ago (U.S. Bureau of Labor Statistics). There could be a carve-out or exception for teens working summer jobs or living with their parents, but Americans working full time and trying to support a family should have the opportunity to make enough to support them. A minimum living wage of $10 per hour could accomplish this, especially since most households are dependent on two wage earners now.

Would the country's economy fall apart if the minimum wage were raised? Not at all, actually just the opposite would happen. An increase would create a broad-based economic revival with enormous secondary benefits. One would expect crime to drop precipitously as the idle poor were put to work at decent wages. Parents would have the resources to properly supervise and educate their children. Teenage pregnancy and drug use would most likely decline immediately.

Would McDonald's suffer? Probably, but not as badly as you might think. It would do what any good capitalist would do—raise prices and maintain profit margins. Because it would be an industrywide change, no one company would be any worse off relative to its competitors. The $.99 menu bacon cheeseburger you buy now at Wendy's would have to increase in price to maybe $1.50. Are you telling me Americans wouldn't vote strongly in favor of this change if they believed it would help the hardest-working poor Americans and help solve some of the country's most intransigent social problems? Free market economists would universally oppose the move as adding unnecessary stickiness to wages. They refuse to see the possibility that the labor market may not be an economically ideal market and ignore the other side benefits such a move could have. They would stress that jobs may be lost, but it is this same group of economists who see the answer to unemployment as eliminating the minimum wage and allowing people to work for next to nothing. Given that many low-wage jobs that are price sensitive have already left for China and Mexico (Source: the Association of Community Organizations for Reform Now, or ACORN), it is not obvious that there would be that much additional job loss from a substantial increase in the minimum wage.

What if health care policy were determined by average Americans rather than HMOs, doctors, and pharmaceutical companies that are the major lobbying forces in the health care debate? Do you think America would have the health problems it has now with 43.6 million uninsured (*United Press International*, 02/10/04), ever-increasing pharmaceutical prices, HMOs that can't be sued, doctors taking kickbacks from drug companies for prescribing their products, and generic drugs that threaten patented drugs prohibited around the world as deaths due to AIDS, tuberculosis, malaria, dehydration, and malnutrition explode?

Health care is a difficult service for free markets to price because people fundamentally object to the idea that the poor receive insufficient care, the rich get better care than most, and even the rich object to a truly free market in which brain surgeons negotiate their fee after they open your head. Many people, especially the elderly, will pay a hefty price not only for cures to illnesses, but for any therapy that might add another year to their lives. But to send America's best and brightest doctors to a search for life-expanding medicines and medical procedures feels much like Ponce de Leon's search for the Fountain of Youth. It seems morally reprehensible to spend so much money to prolong the life of a wealthy octogenarian while many poor Americans cannot enjoy most of the years of their childhood. If Americans knew that 80% of their total lifetime consumption of hospital and medical services occurred in the last two weeks of their lives, they might conclude that it is not only economically wise but compassionate to stop expending so much to keep its most sickly and suffering elderly barely alive. The elderly themselves could make the decision as to when it is appropriate to die, and they could make that decision now by volunteering not to allow expensive life-expanding medical procedures if they face a near-fatal health situation in the future.

While one may be convinced it is necessary to limit the lobbying efforts of corporations, it is more difficult to convince someone that lobbying efforts by citizen-based special interest groups should be constrained. Their ability to contribute money en masse to campaigns should cease. Then when they lobby, it will be the voting power of the citizens they represent that will gain the attention of politicians and not their purchasing power. It might also make sense to insist that laws lobbied into existence by citizen-based special-interest groups be subjected to some kind of confirming national referendum if government-monitored polls show there is general public dissatisfaction with the new proposed legislation.

Even in a world with no lobbyists, there is a general rule for politicians who are campaigning, and that is to never specifically take a position on anything. People against your stated position will remember and vote against you while people in agreement will nod along, but your position will not greatly influence their voting preference. In other words, people seem to remember only bad news. As long as this is the case, it will be very hard to enact any of these cooperative, pain-sharing solutions. Americans must relearn how to cooperate for the greater good, even if it means a bit of short term suffering at the start.

While competition is good for the economic marketplace, cooperation is the key to good government policies. And to cooperate effectively, everyone needs to share the pain to some degree. This will be much easier to do after fairness is instilled back into the system through elimination of undue influence in the government. In such a world, the true greatness of Americans and their generous and cooperative spirit will once again dominate petty politics.

America's Problems Abroad

Ce n'est pas une revolte, c'est une revolution.
FRANCOIS LA ROCHEFOUCAULD-LIANCOURT,
TO LOUIS XVI ON JULY 14, 1789

7

WHY DO THEY HATE US?—WHAT WORLD OPINION COULD TELL AMERICA

America's problems are not limited to domestic issues, the economy, or democratic institutions at home. World opinion has turned decidedly against America, not just among our enemies but also among a number of our allies and much of the developing world. While many Americans' first reaction to criticism from abroad is to become more insular, they need instead to understand and appreciate differing views because such third-party perspectives are less likely to be tainted by self-interests. Certainly, a country like France has its own interests to protect, but when another country is weighing in on a U.S. matter, one would expect these distortive self-interests to be lesser in magnitude than those of a party here in the states that is actively involved in our economy and our politics and has much more to gain. When there is such universal negative opinion concerning America, it cannot be ignored. While our traditional allies' opinions of America are always important, the views held by the developing world are becoming increasingly more significant as they are finally beginning to have a voice on the world stage.

In the past, Americans have decided whether international action was required by asking themselves whether our involvement in an international situation was "in America's interest." Depending how narrowly or broadly one defines America's interest, one can arrive at very different decisions about what actions are warranted. A narrow interpretation would mean involving American personnel and financing only in those situations that would give it an immediate economic, political, or military benefit such as gaining U.S. military bases abroad or accessing new sources of oil and gas. Iraq might be an example of U.S. involvement overseas that satisfies all three of these "narrow" U.S. interests. Controlling Iraq's oil and pipelines satisfied an economic interest, and establishing a military presence in the Middle East put pressure on Iran and Syria to behave. Starting a "wag the dog" type of war served a political necessity, taking the American public's eye off the failed hunt for Osama bin Laden and shifting the emphasis from the weak domestic economy to the war.

A broader understanding of America's interests includes actions that promote world order, reduce poverty and suffering, or reduce conflict and further peace. This is why the promotion of democracy around the world is so important. No other political system has done more to promote peace, stability, and human rights and welfare than democracy. America benefits, as do all the nations of the world, when the planet is more stable and peaceful.

Does the United States have the same moral responsibility to the peoples of the world as it does to its own citizens? The answer is no. The American people have entered into a social contract with their government, have agreed to pay taxes in exchange for basic services and protections, and have accepted the risk of penalties and punishments if they disobey their country's laws and regulations. The American government thus has a much stronger responsibility to Americans than to other peoples of the world who have not agreed to pay our taxes or obey our laws.

Although America's ethical responsibility does indeed extend overseas to its allies and the developing world, it clearly is not as strong a commitment or moral pact as the nation has with its own citizens. Still, it would be shortsighted of America to become involved in global situations only when its actions could be justified solely by its narrowly defined self-interest because many problems in the world require a collective effort to resolve. America's leadership could prove instrumental in finding an answer to these difficulties. If America retreats to its own shores and disengages from international events, the world, and Americans, will be the worse for it.

A simple example of where America can take a more active leading international role is in helping the third world to develop economically. While the immediate benefits of stimulating economic development will accrue to the poor and suffering of the developing countries, America will benefit tremendously from opening new markets for its goods and will gain the respect of the entire world for helping alleviate the human suffering associated with world poverty. This is not to argue that America should just throw more aid dollars at the developing world, but rather, it should work with these countries to see how the introduction of more democratic and properly regulated free market institutions in their countries can lead to greater prosperity and less poverty.

Imagine the developing world's frustration with America's current position as it continues to back dictatorial strongmen, grabs their natural resource wealth, prevents imports into America by means of high tariffs and domestic subsidies, and creates unfair monopolistic positions for foreign companies in these developing countries' basic utility industries such as water and electricity. Argentina, Brazil, and Bolivia have reacted strongly against regimes that they felt were too close to the IMF and American corporate power and not concerned enough with their own people's welfare. In 2000 in Bolivia, price gouging after the public water company had been privatized led to strikes, but it was not until 2003 that Bolivians forcibly removed their leader when he disclosed plans to send their valuable natural gas via pipeline to America (*The New York Times*, 10/17/03). For many Bolivians, this was too close a reminder of the way Spain had seized its silver and gold resources during Bolivia's colonial days.

A poll by Latinobarometer and reported in the November 1, 2003, issue of *The Economist* magazine shows that Latin Americans are becoming disillusioned with the type of democracy practiced in their respective countries. 60% to 90% of the people in each Latin American country responded that they were either "not very satisfied" or "not at all satisfied" with the way democracy works in their country. Each country also reported that it did not find the privatization of state companies to be beneficial. Because these "democratic" Latin governments work so closely with the United States and the IMF to implement governmental institutions and accomplish privatizations, it is only natural that the people direct some of their hatred at America.

America has indeed lost a great deal of respect, not only in the Arab world but now also in much of the remaining Muslim world, Africa, Latin America, and the Far East as well as among many of its traditional allies in Europe. Remember, of the world's 1.2 billion

Muslims only approximately 280 million are Arab. Some Americans are perplexed by this negative change in the world's opinion of their country and ask, "Why do they hate us?"

Conservative American media pundits sometimes say the hatred results because these countries are jealous of America's material success. This is a defense more commonly resorted to by six-year-olds. It shifts the blame effortlessly back to the other party and absolves Americans of the obligation to do any hard thinking or self-examination as to the real cause of the feelings. It is arrogant, too, as the other party comes away believing Americans do not even feel it worthy of any thought or introspection to better understand their objections.

When so many people around the world have a negative view of U.S. policies, Americans should suspect that there might be substance to what they are saying. Different countries hate us for different reasons, but almost without exception, the underlying cause is the same problem discussed throughout this book: The American government's policies do not reflect the views of average Americans but are dominated and controlled by corporate and elitist special interests. Much of the world hates American governmental and economic policy, but not necessarily the American people. American tourists receive a warm reception almost anywhere they travel (with the possible exceptions of Baghdag and North Korea), and America's pop culture—including its movies, music, and blue jeans—are embraced worldwide. The nearly universal appeal of America's pop culture to young people around the world has caused some countries even greater angst as they try to ensure their own culture and art are not swamped by the American pop invasion.

Ask any American on the street what he or she values most about America and you'll most likely hear some of the following words: liberty, freedom, democracy, creativity, opportunity, justice, fairness, and individual spirit. The American people know exactly what makes this country great. But somehow, when America's business and governmental representatives travel to foreign countries, something gets lost in translation.

Almost without exception America's representatives abroad are wealthy elites from government and industry. America appoints ambassadors to other countries based largely on the amount of money they have donated to the latest presidential campaign. This often means it is sending some of the richest and least representative Americans to these countries to speak on our behalf and demonstrate what being American is all about.

Business people also represent America abroad. They travel overseas in droves to enrich themselves and their companies, and unfortunately, because of their sheer power and strength, they often make one-sided deals. They might arrange for the very profitable extraction of precious resources or fight to create foreign monopoly control over local utilities. In any case they make very poor ambassadors of goodwill for America.

It is not just its ambassadors and business people who provide an ugly role model for Americans in the world. Large international aid organizations are increasingly being held in contempt by many in the developing world who believe these groups have done nothing to alleviate poverty and are substantively controlled by America (Easterly, 2001).The world headquarters of the World Bank is chock-full of very well-dressed men and women who appear to spend more time on their wardrobe than on their policy development statements. How could these wealthy elites possibly be effective in solving world poverty?

It is very disturbing to see how the World Bank is organized, funded and managed. It is run by James Wolfensohn, a former investment banker in New York who also headed up Carnegie Hall and The John F. Kennedy Center for the Performing Arts. He reports to a board that is appointed, and after that, all recognizable reporting and responsibility cease. There are no elected officials in the organization. Here, an organization dominated by American and European funding, dedicated to ending poverty and increasing personal freedom in the world, turns out to be the one of the least democratically organized organizations on the planet. Nobel Prize winner Joseph Stiglitz, speaking of his time as chief economist at the World Bank, said, "Decisions were made on the basis of what seemed a curious blend of ideology and bad economics, dogma that sometimes seemed to be thinly veiling special interests .... Open, frank discussion was discouraged—there was no room for it." (Stiglitz, 2002).

And the World Bank is not alone. The other major world aid organization, the IMF, has a similar hierarchical structure with not a single elected representative in the bunch. Many of its country advisors, like those at the World Bank, come from wealthy families, often from economically distressed countries and have little to no business experience. Imagine the president of a poor starving African nation when he is told for the first time that his country advisor from the IMF, who is going to help solve all his economic problems, is from Bogata, Colombia. Many of these country advisors make hundreds of thousands of dollars each year, are exempt from local taxes, and in the greatest of ironies, are not paid in the local currency but in dollars (Easterly, 2001). The irony is that they often recommend a major devaluation of the local currency to stimulate the country's economy, which crushes everybody's take-home pay—that is, everybody's but their own. In his book, *Globalization and Its Discontents,* Joseph Stiglitz writes extensively about the problems caused in the developing world by the IMF.

How successful have the policies of these international aid organizations been? Almost without exception, the nearly 100 countries in which they have instituted antipoverty programs of one kind or another have been miserable failures. For a summary of the ineffectiveness of World Bank programs over the years, please refer to William Easterly's wonderful book, *The Elusive Quest for Growth: Economists' Adventures and Misadventures in the Tropics*. In a funny snapshot of how open the World Bank is to opinion and feedback critical of its work, Easterly wrote this book, used the book's introduction to thank the World Bank for being such an understanding employer and accepting criticism gracefully—and then was fired the next month (Easterly, 2001).

Wouldn't you expect a starving nation to hate America if it sent elitist representatives into their country with advice that was not only extremely painful to follow but almost entirely ineffective? Part of the problem is that almost none of these representatives come from the private sector. They are almost all full-time sycophants of world governments. How could you expect them to preach the gospel of competition and properly regulated free markets, much less have any idea how to encourage new business formation? Of course, it is very difficult to get people with real business experience to dedicate part of their life to helping others less fortunate than themselves halfway around the world.

These pro-government representatives end up recommending big government projects such as dams and roads and funding them with foreign government aid money as long as the first to be repaid are the IMF and World Bank themselves. Government debts get so big financing these zero return projects that future funding drawdowns from international aid organizations go almost exclusively to repaying the IMF and the World Bank. For the first time in decades the IMF this year collected more money than it extended to the developing world. While some infrastructure is required in any country, it makes no sense to saddle a small developing economy with huge debts borrowed to build out highways and dams if the people cannot participate in the economy and proper institutions needed to assure fairness are not in place (Stiglitz, 2002). And you wonder why they hate us?

Many African and Latin American countries now have government debts that exceed 200% of their total GDPs (World Bank 2003). While there is a new movement to try to forgive some of this foreign debt, fully half the developing countries listed in the Bush Administration's initial proposal for debt forgiveness were oligarchies of one kind or another (Larry Diamond's testimony to Congress 2002). This is another form of support to dictatorships, something America morally should not be giving, something that will hurt the local economies, and something that the local citizens will hold against America. And the debt forgiveness programs instituted to date have not required any constraints on future government deficits and borrowings, so it is only a matter of time before these countries are in the same predicament again.

In addition, the IMF supports a completely free market approach that eliminates all government subsidies to farmers and most of those paid to the working poor in the host country (Stiglitz, 2002). Basic requirements like water and electricity not only lose their subsidies but are often privatized to foreign companies, which then exert monopolistic pricing schemes on the local poor. Borders are opened to cheap foreign produced foodstuffs which bankrupt local farmers, unions are discouraged as adding "inflexibility" to wages, and workers are laid off as companies privatize or go bankrupt. Privatizations are totally ineffective as the proceeds go to the corrupt government and not to its citizens and the new private sector companies created operate in a void of good government institutions. If the plan doesn't work, the IMF ensures that foreign investors get their money out first at the cost of additional layoffs for the local workers.

America should work with international organizations rather than act unilaterally around the world. The problem is that the

United Nations also has a long way to go before it can be considered a democratic organization. First, it makes little sense to allow nondemocracies to be represented at the U.N., to serve on important committees, and to have any vote on world issues. Nondemocracies' leaders have no morally justified basis to speak for their people because their people have never had the opportunity to choose their leaders in free and fair open elections. For a Chinese dictator to pretend to speak for his 1.3 billion citizens at the United Nations without having received any sign of legitimacy through elections and no feedback through a free press or civil demonstrations strains the concept of representative government.

Currently, the U.N.'s committee on human rights is chaired by Libya, which won the honor in a 33 to 3 vote (*The New York Times*, 2003). More shocking than having Libya oversee countries' human rights' records is that 33 countries voted in favor of it. In addition, Cuba was just nominated to serve on the human rights committee less than a month after Cuba killed three dissidents and imprisoned over 70 people for fighting for democracy (*The New York Times*, 4/24/03). Although the U.N. is not controlled by America, America clearly would have to take the lead if any pro-democracy movement were to be initiated within the U.N. Ideally, a new international organization could be formed and composed of just the democracies of the world. This would be the proper vehicle for deciding human rights violations around the world or for applying force if it became necessary to remove a brutal dictator from power.

And what of America's international policies? Are they reflective of the average American's view of justice and democracy, or have they been co-opted by special interests to reflect their own greedy self-serving pursuit of power and profit?

The great gifts that America has to offer the world are democracy and properly regulated free market capitalism. Through aggressive implementation of both institutions, the world has the chance to dramatically increase its economic growth and drastically reduce poverty in the next 60 years. Problems cannot be solved immediately because time must be given for countries to have a chance to grow themselves out of poverty, but real growth rates of 5% to 10% per year are not unachievable (Roll and Talbott, 2003). At such a real growth rate, poverty can be eliminated essentially in many developing countries in our lifetime. Infant mortality can be dramatically reduced, life expectancies increased, health care improved, education made affordable, pollution abated, and government and elitist corruption ended (Barro, 1996). And yet America's current international policies have little to do with fulfilling these basic democratic and institutional needs.

Why does America end up supporting dictators and autocrats around the world? Economists have found that countries with strong natural resources are more likely to be dictatorial and grow more slowly (Sachs and Warner, 2000) because autocrats can fund their activities through the foreign sale of a country's gold, diamonds, or oil and gas. They thus have no need to build a healthy broad-based growing economy. Unfortunately, American oil and gas or mining companies are very likely to support a dictatorship because it makes the natural resource extraction and sale that much easier and more profitable. U.S. oil companies are in Nigeria, its mineral companies are in Indonesia, and its diamond and mining companies are in Sierra Leone. Under lobbying pressure, the American government ends up supporting its largest natural resource companies and quickly becomes an ally of the dictator's regime and an enemy of his people.

Could America's trade policies be partially responsible for the intense dislike of America expressed by many peoples of the world? Many Americans believe, at least theoretically, in open borders, free international trade, no tariffs, and no trade quotas. Theoretically,

America is guided by the theory of comparative advantage that says that everybody benefits by international trade, even a less productive country that trades with a more productive one. But in a world of free migration of people, work skills, and ideas, the value added suggested by the theory of comparative trade may be dramatically overstated. Much of the value of open borders may instead come from imposing international standards of transparency and openness on corrupt businesses and dishonest developing country governments.

In reality, America forces open borders and open trade on members of the developing world by demanding they join the WTO. The WTO is an extremely undemocratic organization with appointed, not elected, officials speaking supposedly on behalf of their respective countries in closed meetings, without publicity, and now, due to street protesters at previous meetings, in fairly inaccessible locations. The policies of the WTO are biased strongly toward business, and the organization has refused to allow meaningful participation by environmentalists or labor representatives (Greider, 1997).

But, the pro-business agenda of the WTO is not the most offensive part of its trade policy for the developing world. While the WTO is a supposed international organization, American free marketers were strongly behind its creation, and the third world believes it is controlled by the advanced countries, especially the U.S. Having forced these countries to open their borders to its goods, America effectively keeps its borders closed to theirs. America provides hundreds of billions of dollars in subsidies to its large industrial agribusiness companies and passes high restrictive tariffs to protect U.S. textile interests at home. America has stringent consumer regulations, making it almost impossible for any third-world country's food products to pass its inspections and requirements for import (Greider, 1997).

When you force open a developing country to trade, it is assumed that the developed world will end up selling all the autos, computers, machinery, and technical equipment in town. The quid pro quo, and the only chance for employment and nonstarvation wages in the developing country, is that it will have the opportunity to sell labor-intensive goods like textiles, footwear, and some agricultural products back to the advanced countries. If the advanced countries cut off this trade, poverty will explode. This is exactly the case in almost all of Africa and much of South America. Incomes have plummeted in most of Latin America, and in Africa the real average per capita income has dropped precipitously from approximately $2,500 twenty years ago to just over $750 (Maddison, 2001). No American citizen would be in favor of such one-sided trade, but that is our country's policy, and that is another reason other countries hate us.

Many believe the comparative advantage of mostly agrarian low-skilled developing countries is by definition in agriculture. If this is true, these countries are damned for all time to be the poor breadbaskets of the modern world, with low-tech workers toiling long hot days in the field and earning meager wages. The World Bank's conferences on African development are full of economists making presentations about how Africa could farm more efficiently, even though little real capital investment is available for farm machinery. But in so doing, the World Bank is dooming Africa to meager per capita incomes in the $1,000 to $2,000 range because it is almost impossible to earn any greater wage on a labor-intensive farm that must compete with the capital-intensive agribusiness's low-cost imported foodstuffs. Globally speaking in today's high tech world, agriculture is a capital-intensive business, and asking labor-intensive economies prevalent in the developing world to focus on it ensures their citizens will never escape poverty.

The alternative to staying down home on the farm is not very encouraging either. Farmers in these open-border developing countries are often bankrupted by the cheap importing of big agribusiness food and end up moving to the cities in search of work. This is a daunting prospect because they are joined in the growing cities of China or Mexico or Brazil by tens of millions of unemployed farmers facing similar circumstances (Greider, 1997). Although migration from the farm to the city is a natural occurrence during industrialization, in developing countries, the necessary capital to build factories in the cities is often just not there. It is not as if great industrial opportunities in the city drew farmers off their land. Rather, cheap imported food forced them off their land before their country's industrial policy was sufficiently established to provide jobs in the city. As a result, numerous cities around the world—including Mexico City, Calcutta, Capetown, Rio de Janeiro, and Beijing—have hundreds of millions of peasants starving on their streets with no chance for meaningful work in the foreseeable future. Do you think the conversation on the poor streets of these cities ever turns to how much they hate America?

In addition to trade policy, many of America's international diplomatic policies have seemed far from fair and just. America encourages developing countries to stop cutting timber from their forests, stop degrading their wetlands, and stop polluting their water and air. And yet it encourages its own dirtiest coal-fired utilities in America not only to keep burning coal but also to expand their operations. America is one of the few countries in the world that has not signed the Kyoto Protocol treaty that tries to contain global warming (*The New York Times,* 4/10/03). America's industrialists know that to contain global warming, it must restrict the burning of fossil fuels, especially coal. To them, this smells of restricting growth, absolutely forbidden by the stock market crowd. Everyone knows that America consumes more power per person and creates more waste per person than any country on earth. America pressures Brazil to quit cutting its rainforest, and yet America, during its economic development, cut down nearly 95% of its woodlands.

In addition to refusing to sign the Kyoto Protocol treaty, the United States refused to sign an international agreement to set up a world court for trying international war criminals. The Bush administration, fearing that a politicized international prosecutor could indict American officials or military personnel for "crimes" committed during American conflicts abroad, has actively campaigned against the institution (*The New York Times*, 3/12/03). To the rest of the world this just smells of imperialism.

Just as America supports dictators around the world and opposes popular democratic uprisings, so also, to support its largest companies, it often leads the fight against organizing labor and bringing a better life to the world's workers. Each time a developing country tries to improve its workers' welfare by allowing unionization, America's biggest corporations simply pick up and move to the next non-union country. American corporations picked their way across the nations of the South Pacific in this way, moving from the Philippines to Malaysia to Thailand, finally ending up in Vietnam and China. China is ideal from the American industrialists' perspective because it arrests and jails union organizers. The damage done by China's anti-union stance has not just been limited to low wages in that country. With hundreds of millions of Chinese working for less than $1 per day (World Bank 2002), this prohibition on union organizing in China puts a cap on what other unskilled workers around the world can earn. Unskilled workers in Africa and South America must compete for wages against intentionally non-organized Chinese workers. What could they possibly produce that China couldn't or isn't producing more cheaply already with its guaranteed low wages?

There is one more important reason that the world is uneasy with America—war! If the American administration is perceived as hawkish in preferring wars rather than international reconciliation to settle international disputes, much of the hatred felt toward the American government might be deserved. Most of the American people, it turns out, are extremely peace loving. The reason that democracies rarely fight each other is that in these countries, the citizens who will actually have to bear the cost of war have a real say in whether they go to war (Roll and Talbott, 2003)

Lately, it seems as though America's leaders are much more aggressive militarily than are their citizens. Americans typically end up supporting their leaders' militaristic conquests in the end, but most of this support could be due to general patriotism or a pro-administration media. But recently, American leaders have been initiating many conflicts, even going so far as to start preemptive wars. The leaders conducting this policy may feel in their hearts that they are doing the right thing. The moral concept behind a country's democracy is that no one person can make such a decision without consulting the country's citizens or their representatives. In the case of international war, the world's other democracies should be consulted to ensure that the action by the aggressor country is morally defendable. The reason democracy works is that even megalomaniacs, who are convinced of the rightness and justness of their actions, must seek approval from a majority of their citizens or representatives before taking major actions to ensure that they are not deluding themselves. If it were not for this majority check on morals and rationality, any individual could conduct any offense, regardless of how unjust or immoral it might be, and still try to claim the moral high ground (W. Talbott, 2004). Didn't Britain always believe it had India's best interests at heart when it continued to subject Indians to British rule? A commanding officer in Vietnam believed he had to burn a

Vietnamese village in order to save it. Who ever went to war to fight for an unjust or immoral cause? Don't both sides in an armed conflict typically claim God is on their side?

This pro-war stance of America's leaders is a direct result of the democratic processes breaking up at home. There is nothing better than being the leader of a country that has a broken system of democracy. There literally is no one to answer to. You might get a bit arrogant and egotistical if you commanded the world's strongest army but did not have to report to the fathers and mothers of those brave fighting men and women who were laying down their lives for your war. The concept of "might is right," a fundamental philosophy of any imperialist, can easily be traced to unbridled and untamed egotistical leaders.

One might think that industry itself would act to restrain a country's military ambitions as it is difficult to trade and conduct international business during war, but business itself is split between consumer industries and the defense establishment. As World War II showed, there is nothing like a good war to pull a country out of a depression. If democracy were working properly, much greater weight would be given to the families of the soldiers who have to fight these conflicts and much greater human emphasis would be placed on the lives lost by the opposition. Such sympathy for the enemy comes from human, not corporate or governmental interests. If the American people had better control over their military and their government, the world would have a lot less to hate about us.

If part of a well-functioning democracy is keeping the electorate informed of the facts so that it can make intelligent decisions, something has gone wrong because Americans were kept pretty much in the dark when it came to the invasion of Iraq. The reasons that were given for the invasion included removing weapons of mass destruction that threatened the U.S. and punishing Iraq for their supposed involvement in 9/11 (*The New York Times,* 2003). Neither of these suppositions has been proven. It seems that the U.S. president now believes it is his right to simply package a marketing presentation to the American people. This way, he expects to convince them to take a particular action he has already decided to pursue rather than fully disclose all appropriate and available information and leave the decision making up to them.

America's international relations problems are not confined to its enemies or the developing world. Recently, America lost the support of even its life-long European allies. The battle is about whether America will abide by international rules of order and conduct its international actions through consultation with its allies or take the "might is right" imperialistic approach and decide alone what action is needed internationally to protect its "self-interest". The damage America suffers by losing the trust of the world community is not readily apparent to a fairly isolated imperialist, but the time will come when America needs the support and goodwill of its friends, and the government will have frittered it away. And to think this has all occurred so shortly after 9/11, when Americans can still recall listening to the Star Spangled Banner being sung by tens of thousands of French citizens marching up the Champs-Elysees.

So when you are asked, "Why do they hate us?" maybe now you can respond with another question: "Why don't they hate us even more?" Until Americans get control of their democracy and get their government's policies and businesses' activities to better reflect their own belief systems, they will always be rightfully subjected to criticism from their neighbors in the world who are made to bear the brunt of their narrow-minded and undemocratic actions. America's faults, which it either seems to be oblivious to or chooses to ignore, seem to be readily apparent to the 5.7 billion non-Americans that it shares this planet with.

8

MORE DEMOCRACY IS THE ANSWER

Many of the reasons that the world distrusts America can be traced back to America's own dysfunctional democratic institutions. America's role in the world has been misguided by a government that poorly reflects its citizens' values and beliefs. Therefore, this discussion will concern the proper role America should be playing in the developing world as it represents nearly five-sixths of the world's population, or over five billion people. And one billion of these are trying to live on average incomes of less than $1 per day.

What should America be doing to improve the well-being of the world's people? Just as at home, the key to its actions in the rest of the world is supporting democracy around the world. Only by allowing indigenous local people effective control over their lives, their economies, and their governments can Americans reasonably expect peaceful coexistence in the world.

Supporting democracy is not always easy. While guided by a general policy of non-interference, America faces the difficult question of what to do about dictatorships in which millions of people are suffering not only human rights abuses, but also hunger and poverty. Is outside intervention justified to stop the deadly coercion of a dictator? What is it about democracy that might improve the economies of the developing world and allow its citizens to grow out of poverty and despair? Democracy may not only be the answer to what ails America, it might also provide the key to alleviating the suffering of people in the developing world. The challenge is two-fold. How do peace loving democracies deal effectively with ruthless dictators who are abusing their peoples? And how can advanced countries have a positive impact on developing countries without violating the self-determination requisite of a democratic form of government they will be promoting? Is it ethical to force democracy on a starving dictatorship?

We have seen that wealthier countries seem to be more democratic and that poorer countries typically are more politically repressive. Although in our research, economic liberalization through property rights and enforceable contracts appeared to be even more important to prosperity than political liberalization (the vote, freedom of the press, civil liberties), there is no denying that these democratic institutions also played an important role (Roll and Talbott, 2003). A fairly sophisticated statistical approach was utilized in this academic research to ensure that it was indeed greater democracy and not some other factor that was correlating well with higher country incomes, but a more simplistic approach makes the same point.

If you think of where on the map the poorest countries of the world are located and where the wealthiest countries are, you can make some very general statements about democracy and the wealth of nations. First, the wealthiest nations are primarily in Europe, North America, and Australia, all democratic strongholds. Great wealth has also been created in recent history in Japan, South Korea, Singapore, and Taiwan. Although not necessarily ideally democratic when they started their development, each of these countries became more democratic as it developed further. All were led by individuals or parties who seemed to have their people's best interest at heart and thus enacted the type of economic and institutional reforms conducive to growth.

An examination of where the poorest countries are located on the map of the world finds them in areas short of true democracy. The poorest countries include much of the former Soviet bloc—which only now is beginning to enjoy freedom and economic growth—communist China, and communist Southeast Asia, the dictatorships of the Middle East and Africa and Latin America. Communist China has recently begun to enjoy high economic growth, but it did so through the introduction of free market reforms. A pessimist in China would argue that the country's output per person is still quite low (World Bank 2002) and that without the self-policing of government inherent in democracies, the country might be doomed for a reversal of fortune. Already, S&P estimates that fully 45% of the loans held by Chinese banks are nonperforming (*Business Week*, 10/6/03). This is a typical problem in an autocracy because bank debt is extended not based on credit quality judgments but often on the say-so of a high ranking government official.

Many of the relatively poor countries in Africa and Latin America are actually quite new democracies. It is too soon to tell whether democratic reforms in Africa's relatively new democracies are working. If they are democratic in name only, in an attempt to placate aid providers and trade organizations, they are probably doomed to fail economically.

The more established, but poor, democracies of Latin America pose a more interesting question. Countries like Chile have not been democratic long enough to acquire great wealth, but their improved growth rates should yield higher incomes in the future. Can democratic forms of government in countries like Argentina and Brazil truly represent all the people when a small minority in each country controls most of the wealth and resources? Argentina had a "bloodless revolution" in 2001, but two years later the top three finishers in their presidential primary were all members of the same political party that had gotten the country into financial problems to begin with. It is hard to have true democracy without at least two viable political parties.

So both a sophisticated statistical regression and a very simple back-of-the-envelope approach yield the same conclusion: Democracy and prosperity seem to travel together. But why? A clue is offered by Nobel Prize winner Amartya Sen who posited that no democracy has ever suffered a famine (Sen, 1981 and 1999). Now the record on democracies relative to all of human history is still quite new, but it is a remarkable statement, especially coming from a native of India, a democratic country that has had great trouble feeding its enormous population. In understanding this simple statement, one can begin to understand the power of democracy in promoting the welfare of the people.

First, Sen argued that famines were economic events, not related to nature or weather. Droughts are weather-related events, but not all droughts result in famines. Sen showed that famines in agrarian societies result not because of a lack of food, but for a lack of income. The poor worker in an agrarian economy typically works on a farm or in the distribution of crops and livestock.

Therefore, when a drought occurs, it reduces the job opportunities and income available to the farm workers, thus lowering their incomes. Although food is still available, the workers whose incomes are tied to the farm economy can no longer afford to purchase it and they begin to starve. In the most extreme cases, a famine results, often with substantial food supplies still on the shelf but out of the reach of the agrarian worker's depressed earnings.

Sen's startling conclusion about democracies' ability to prevent famines can be understood only if one understands the economic benefits of democracy. A major economic benefit of a well-functioning democracy is that it provides valuable feedback to a country's leaders about the general welfare of the people. In the long run, people vote, which is a powerful, and sometimes fatal, feedback mechanism to government leaders. Over a shorter time horizon, however, a free press and the rights of free assembly and speech ensure that government leaders will be acutely aware not only of any serious problems affecting the welfare of the electorate, but also of the current administration's performance.

Consider life in a dictatorship. The people are punished if they object to any government policy. The dictator typically surrounds himself with "yes men" who tell him what he wants to hear. The media does not expose problems but rather is used as a propaganda tool to quell any civil unrest. There is no feedback to the dictator. All information flow is strictly downhill, from him to his subjects. The dictatorship of Saddam Hussein in Iraq is a wonderful example. All Saddam's minions were constantly spouting the party line, the state-run television was used solely to distribute lies and propaganda, and Iraq's minister of information's misstatements denying that the U.S. Army was indeed at the Bhagdad airport during the Iraq conflict sounded like something out of the novel *1984*.

We spoke earlier of an equally important function that democratic institutions provide, and that is to act as a self-policing mechanism. What self-policing is a dictator subject to? He can pretty much do whatever he wishes, and if he fails, there are no repercussions. In a democracy, the people can speak out against government excess and abuse, and if not satisfied, they can exercise the strongest policing action; they can vote the incumbents out of office.

When presented with the evidence that democratic reforms can lead to economic prosperity, skeptics typically raise the same question: "What about Singapore?" Singapore, a true growth superstar, on paper was always a democracy, but in actuality was an autocracy with Lee Kuan Yew serving as prime minister. While sham elections were held, any opponents who criticized Lee Kuan Yew's record or started to gain the support of voters were sued by Lee Kuan Yew for slander and forced to resign (W. Talbott, 2004). Thus, we see the importance in the U.S. of not having slander rules apply to disclosures about public figures.

How then did Singapore experience remarkable economic growth over the last 50 years? In fairness, it is not just Singapore that developed rapidly without true democracy. South Korea and Taiwan also made rapid progress economically before implementing full-scale two-party democracy. China today is growing at approximately 10% per year (World Bank 2002) with only very modest democratic reform. One could argue that Nazi Germany, Stalin's Russia, and Mao's China temporarily also made incredible economic progress without a hint of democracy. While living conditions in these countries may have been horrific, economic progress, measured solely in terms of GDP growth, was very positive as Hitler prepared for war and Stalin and Mao industrialized.

It seems these economically "successful" dictatorships were of two kinds. Some, like Singapore, would be called benevolent dictatorships as their leaders, while not facing real political pressure, still acted mostly in the best interests of their people. The second group includes countries such as Stalin's Russia and Mao's China. There was nothing benevolent about their rule. Economic growth occurred but only because the leaders forced the populations to industrialize, labor, and save rather than consume. GDP increased, but the quality of life suffered. While infant mortality declined, people lived a harsh life of brutal work and in terrible conditions. In each country, famines took tens of millions of people, specifically because they did not have the democratic feedback mechanisms mentioned earlier by Sen, and it is not clear their ruthless leaders would have cared much even if they did.

Clearly, these types of repressive regimes are not the model people reference when speaking of dictatorships that might achieve economic growth. These repressive systems were very unstable and eventually collapsed. It is interesting that at the time, many argued that a country needs a strong dictator to achieve a stable rule of law in which industry can flourish. This does not have to be the case. A well-organized constitutional democracy can provide the same stability and rule of law necessary for commerce without giving up important and valuable individual freedoms (De Vanssay and Spindler, 1992).

I do believe that strict dictatorships have one economic advantage over very young democracies. When developing countries are first industrializing, they go through enormous economic dislocations as the predominately agrarian society evolves into one based on industry. Specifically, local farmers go bankrupt as larger agribusinesses move in and crop prices drop, and the farmers move to the city where they find few jobs and lots of other displaced out-of-work farmers. Although this may seem to be a necessary evil first step in the march to development, many young democracies are hesitant to take it. Under economic pressures, the displaced farm work force becomes a potent political voice that can, and sometimes does, stall necessary economic reform. If dictatorial regimes have any competitive advantage over democracies in the early stages of development, it is in their ability to push a country and its people past this difficult first stage of industrialization by ignoring the short-term complaints of their citizenry. Such a minor benefit is dwarfed by the enormous pain and cost that a dictatorship exacts from its people in the long run.

What about China today? Which camp does it fall into? Some would argue that its dramatic growth is pulling China's citizens out of poverty, so there must be some benevolence to that. Others would be less sanguine. They would point to the repression that still occurs today and the terrible living conditions of many of its workers. The fact that there is no free press makes observation difficult. Union organizing is outlawed. Preventing workers from organizing is a Stalinist tactic to ensure that workers' complaints are never voiced. Wages, working conditions, and living arrangements for employees can all be abused without any feedback from the workers. In such a system, what sense does it make to talk about benevolence?

The jury is still out on China. Its reported growth rates, while impressive, spring from a very small base. Ten percent growth when the average income is $2,700 per person is less impressive than 4% growth in an advanced democratic economy with an average income of $35,000. And because China is a closed society, there is no way to check whether the economic growth statistics it is reporting are indeed accurate. There are already suggestions from some that the numbers just don't add up and some kind of phony accounting might have been implemented.

I recently visited The Kingdom of Jordan at the invitation of the Royal Economics Minister. I was struck by how much effort was being made by the king and his government to try to stimulate growth in Jordan's economy. They were doing everything, that is, short of stimulating real democratic reform. But using Singapore as a model and having what seemed to me like the best of intentions, the king was honestly trying very hard to improve the economic lives of his people through benevolence rather than democratic reform. He had opened free trade zones with the U.S., joined the WTO and General Agreement on Tariffs and Trade (GATT), opened his borders to international trade, and verbally encouraged entrepreneurship and new business formation. The World Bank and USAID often held Jordan up as a role model for the entire Middle East. And the result of all these good works by the king— exactly zero growth in his people's real per capita incomes for the last 20 years.

What went wrong? Or alternatively, "What is wrong with a benevolent dictator?" First, the problem with any dictator is that there is only one world view—his! Unlike a democracy in which policy ideas are debated and—it is hoped—improved, a dictator's ideas are just enacted. So what happens? One of two things occurs. If the dictator is truly benevolent, wise, well educated in economics, and a good student of other successful economies, he enacts the kind of economic reforms spoken of earlier. Namely, he initiates a strong rule of law, strong property rights, elimination of corruption and burdensome regulation, and active encouragement of private sector growth while minimizing the negative impact of government.

But in a world of little to no debate, it is much more likely that even a well-meaning dictator might apply the wrong recipe to his economy. And why is a well-intentioned dictator bad for an economy? Because he will never receive the necessary feedback he needs to make corrections to his policies; he will never be voted out of office by unemployed citizens, and journalists will never criticize his efforts because he controls the newspapers. He will never look out his window and see people protesting in the streets. The leaders of the opposition party will not be creating a rival economic plan because there is no opposition party. And worst, his own advisors will be afraid of raising any criticism of the plan for fear of suffering his wrath. Their livelihoods depend on how much they please their sovereign.

A benevolent dictator has other shortcomings in addition to poor feedback mechanisms on policies and objectives. He is naturally biased against making the type of free market reforms that are essential for a growing economy. By definition, his is a government office, so he would have to be truly benevolent to reduce the power of the state and encourage a shift in power to the private sector. This is the primary reason dictatorial regimes languish with little real economic growth. They refuse to give up power and control to the marketplace. What good is it to be dictator if you can't create monopolistic cartels for your relatives and conduct sham banking and foreign currency transactions for your friends? If you can't manipulate the economy, what is the payoff to being dictator?

Assuming there is a truly benevolent dictator who is knowledgeable enough to try to enact free market reforms and the institutions necessary to implement them, what might go wrong? Here I will return to my experience in Jordan. I would describe the entire economic decision-making process in Jordan as top-down. The king decides what policies might stimulate the economy, and then his advisors are charged with implementing his decisions. This is not too different from the way American corporate CEOs or American football coaches implement their respective game plans. The reason most football teams run well as dictatorships is that everyone on the team understands and shares the same goals, and everyone clearly understands the rules. Corporations also have fairly straightforward shared objectives and goals of maximizing shareholder value, and they have the benefit of instant feedback from shareholders as their stock trades actively at free-floating prices. Countries are quite a different story. They are composed of people of varying backgrounds, beliefs, goals, and ambitions. One person alone at the top could hardly pretend to speak for all or make decisions that reflect everyone's desires and needs.

Bottom-up decision making is a better form of reaching consensus and optimal decisions properly reflecting everybody's input. It just so happens that healthy, growing economies also are bottom-up. A vibrant economy is one in which all a country's citizens are maximizing their efforts. To encourage growth, one would want the full participation of everyone in the economy and should encourage entrepreneurship in every facet of a country's policies. Therefore, there is a basic disconnect between dictatorial top-down decision making and the inclusive bottom-up competitive economy most conducive to growth.

In Jordan, the king was very busy each day meeting with Microsoft or NHK trying to promote business in his kingdom. But I got the sense that the rest of the country was sitting and waiting to see what the king would accomplish in his meetings. This generated an incredible aura of passivity, which is not the best characteristic for a hard-charging economy. The problem with paternalism is it encourages inactivity in the citizenry. Also, there were only so many hours in the king's day in which to hold meetings with prospective investors and business partners, so economic progress was limited. This is an extreme case, but it makes the point of how important bottom-up economies are. The king had room for eight one-hour business meetings in a day, but because the business community depended on him so completely, they were not setting up the millions of business meetings of their own with the millions of manhours available to them in any one day.

Another problem with top-down economic management is that it can be very exclusionary. Entire groups can be left out of the planning because the king may not understand their wish to participate or may judge them to have little worth. In Jordan, as in most Islamic societies, women are well educated but terribly underutilized in the workforce. In addition, Jordan has a unique problem. Nearly half its population is displaced Palestinians, many living in internment camps, some for 50 years or more. In top-down planning, a king can assume it is better for women to stay at home or for Palestinians to be cared for in internment camps funded by international donations. Bottom-up economies have no such implied or accidental discrimination or exclusion. Whoever wants to work works. People make their own decisions. Women work in the United States for the same reasons men do—they need to, they enjoy it, or both, and it is their decision.

How else do so-called benevolent dictators go wrong? First, just because they are benevolent today does not ensure their benevolence in the future. Once you surrender your civil rights, it is difficult to reclaim them if the dictator's aspirations become less benevolent. Or if his policies turn out to be less effective than expected. Worse, there is no guarantee that his chosen successor will also be benevolent. Second, allowing some leaders to hide comfortably behind the screen of benevolence encourages all dictators, regardless of the brutality of their regimes, to also claim the benevolent title.

So how do we explain Singapore? The dictator, Lee Kuan Yew, appeared to be truly benevolent, economically speaking, and very smart. While he did not have adequate feedback from his own populace concerning the effectiveness of his policies, he benefited tremendously from feedback from other countries that had enacted successful reforms. To some extent, he piggybacked on the feedback and success of the world's wealthier democracies.

He was also very lucky. The programs he emphasized, such as exports and the high-tech sector, turned out to be good bets. But unlike a well-diversified democratic economy in which many entrepreneurs are making bets in various industries and products,

Singapore put all its eggs in one basket. If Lee Kuan Yew had been wrong, his country would have suffered terribly. Although his decision to have a very small government appears in hindsight to be efficient, one may have come to a different conclusion if his people had to weather a 1930s-type depression without adequate governmental social safety nets.

Autocratic regimes, including supposed "benevolent" dictatorships, are therefore less conducive to economic growth than democracies. It should be absolutely clear that democracy is the preferred regime type, not only for individual liberties and freedoms, but also for economic growth. There is no required trade-off. You can have the freedom of democracy, and it can generate excellent economic growth and prosperity (Roll and Talbott, 2003).

Because five-sixths of the population of the world lives in poverty, economic growth is a prerequisite for freedom. Sen argues in his book *Development as Freedom* that greater freedom is the proper measure of a country's and its people's development. But he also argues that it is difficult to gain individual freedoms without economic development. In a developing economy in which most of the citizens spend the majority of their time fulfilling their most basic food, clothing, and shelter needs, what sense does it make to talk about individual liberties and freedoms without further economic growth. It is only through greater economic productivity that individuals acquire the freedom to pursue individual pleasures such as writing, reading, education, sports, the arts, music, hobbies, and spending time with family and friends.

Economic prosperity also brings societies the opportunities to spend monies on environmental causes, public education, health care, and care for the poor, elderly, and disabled. While many in the environmental movement believe economic growth damages the environment, they do not properly weigh the ability of wealthy countries to clean up their environmental problems by spending on pollution control systems. The former Soviet Union and the eastern bloc countries were infamous for polluted rivers and darkened polluted skies (*Environment,* December 1988) whereas poor Latin American countries are rapidly damaging their environment by cutting and burning the trees of the Amazon (*Newsweek,* 9/2/02). It seems unfair to ask developing countries to absorb costly environmental charges while they are jump-starting their economies, especially as the advanced countries did not do so until much further along in their development. Advanced countries clearly consume more and create more waste, but they have the economic resources to do something about it.

To come back to the question whether America should export democracy and economic development to the third world, the moral answer is a resounding *yes.* Given its knowledge of how to create economic wealth and given the pain many in the developing world are suffering under brutal dictatorships, America has a moral obligation to intercede. Many believe America should not intercede in the affairs of other nations unless it is in its best interest. This argument illogically extends Adam Smith's argument of self-interest to an international arena. There is no theoretical basis to believe societies will be better off if they act only in their narrow self interest. Many of these societies in the developing world are fairly closed societies with no international trade to speak of. Because Americans never hear much from them makes their problems easier for Americans to ignore.

But, you might ask, don't brutal dictatorships have a right to country sovereignty? Shouldn't countries maintain world stability by keeping out of the domestic affairs of other nations, even brutal dictatorships?

If dictators do claim country sovereignty, where does this right come from? Historically, kings claimed their sovereign powers were derived from God. Today, moral authority to rule comes from the people themselves. But dictators have no such authority granted by their people. Their governments, by definition, are immoral, regardless of how benevolent they might appear to be. Without the vote and confidence of their people, dictatorships cannot pretend to represent the people's interests. Unless popular elections were required to achieve moral leadership, any dictator could claim benevolent status and ethical leadership. As discussed previously, many immoral dictators do exactly this. They claim everything they do is in their people's interest but still fail to test that theory with a popular election.

So, dictators depend for their existence on the non-interference in their country's affairs by the democratically elected governments of the world. Following this argument, countries of the free world, by their complacency and limited self-interest, are morally the equivalent of co-conspirators with the dictators of the world in denying the citizens brutalized by the dictators the opportunities and freedoms associated with democracy and economic development.

Now ethicists might argue that moral requirements could not demand that a nation act proactively and take added risk to do good for others. But the same ethicists might be shocked at how little is being done in the world on behalf of those suffering under dictatorship. Their arguments for non-interference might be strained by the fact that millions are dying of starvation and torture under these dictatorial regimes. What is the difference between Hitler's persecution and murder of Jews in Germany in World War II and the starvation and oppression of millions of North Koreans today? It is now clear that famines are man-made economic events typically resulting from autocrats ignoring the pleas of their citizens. Thousands, if not tens of thousands, of children are being tortured and murdered in North Korea, many the sons and daughters of refugee Korean women returning to North Korea having fathered children with Chinese fathers.

The problem of intervention is complicated by the fact that dictators are often quite brutal and do not respond to well-intentioned, pacifist half-measures. Also, to prevent nations from using the pretense of liberating people from dictatorship to disguise self-interested invasions, it seems reasonable to demand that any physical intervention should have support from majority of the democratic nations of the world.

What reasonably can be done?

Human rights and human dignity should be emphasized in all of the work with the developing world. An emphasis on human rights is a stone's throw from promoting the basic tenets of democracy, and promoting the dignity of every human being is the most important ingredient to the proper functioning of a civil society. Until people, especially women, in the developing world come to believe that their lives and opinions matter, there will be little progress toward democratic reform.

In addition, the world should cut off all aid, trade, and arms to dictatorships. No aid, trade, or arms (NATA, pronounced *nada* as in nothing) may not be totally effective in displacing dictators, but it should put maximum pressure on their regimes and at least prevent them from continuing to grow or threaten their neighbors militarily. Again, such a movement would have maximum benefit if implemented by an international organization representing all the democracies of the world. Because this would cause suffering of the innocent population it should only be implemented for a short period of time in concert with other, more serious measures.

China, for instance, is a pure dictatorship. Religious believers are persecuted, government reformers are tortured, and labor organizers are imprisoned. Many choose to conduct trade with China in hopes that including the Chinese in the world community will eventually put pressure on the government to reform. Some also argue that economic development, even in a dictatorship, will lessen some of the suffering of the people of China.

What is wrong with such trade? Although China is not currently a military threat to the U.S., if it continues to grow at close to 10% a year, it is not unfathomable, given its enormous population, that China could afford a bigger military budget than could the U.S. in as little as 10 years. Only then, when it will be too late, will China's true aspirations with regard to Taiwan, Mongolia, Tibet, and the world be disclosed. Once again, America will be criticized for having created its own worst enemy.

Even if we ignore the potential military threat, China's anti-labor policies pose a real threat to world stability. Because China's workers typically earn less than $1 per day and do not have the opportunity to organize to fight for better pay and working conditions, they set an incredibly low standard for the rest of the world's workers to match. If you are trying to develop an export-led economy in a developing country, what can you export more cheaply than China that will provide a reasonable level of income and welfare for your citizens? Regardless of how much you devalue your currency, competing with hundreds of millions of $1-per-day workers is a daunting prospect. China's competitive power in the world marketplace is so dominant that it may explain the poor growth prospects of many developing countries in Africa and Latin America that have taken their economic medicine, opened borders, encouraged trade and growth, but still languish among the poorest countries on the planet. So in deciding to trade with a dictatorial regime like China, America may have damned the poorest people of the world to lives of poverty and despair.

The difficulty in cutting off trade and aid is that some humanitarian relief must still be pursued, and this is often misdirected by the dictatorship (Easterly, 1993). Distribution of humanitarian aid to a dictatorship should be supervised on the ground by international organizations. If the dictator prevents this oversight, it should be a very serious reason for the international community to consider more serious alternatives with regard to that country's leadership.

I can envision a new community of democracies, similar to the European Common Market, that trades only with other democracies and on very favorable tariff and trade terms. To gain admittance requires a country become a democracy. Just such a "democracies only" club could eventually replace the U.N. as the major international arbiter if the U.N. does not pursue reforms to make its membership more democratic and thus more morally justified in its decisions.

What happens once dictatorships are isolated? It will be to the world's benefit because their economic prospects will be quite limited due to their lack of democratic input. Some may prosper by benevolently doing what is best for their citizens, but these countries will be in the minority. America must be concerned about the most brutal, the most repressive, and the most economically backward because no matter how much one would like to introduce human rights campaigns and voting rights into these countries, their dictators would recognize the threat of such an outside influence and prevent it. Therefore, America's choices are somewhat limited. What are they?

America can do nothing and share the moral blame for the suffering of millions. Or it can cut off aid, trade and arms and hope internal revolt will foment, but given the unequal distribution of weaponry in most regimes, that is not likely to happen. Finally, America might approach this newly formed community of democracies and achieve the moral authority it needs to authorize an assassination of the dictator or launch a liberating invasion. Invasions and assassinations, even when world sanctioned, seem an ethical stretch. But to those who think it is immoral to remove a brutal dictator through force, suppose one of your relatives; your father, your mother, your child, was among the millions dying in the dictator's country from famine, repression or torture. Now imagine if every one of the millions who are suffering were your relations.

There are obvious problems with the use of force. First, any preemptive use of force only seems to set ugly precedents for others in solving their problems with their neighbors. Second, a grand battle of rich country versus poor dictatorship will probably only result in the deaths of many innocent conscripted soldiers who have no incentive to fight on behalf of their dictator. Finally, the damage done to a country's infrastructure and civilian population may produce more hardship than an impoverished nation can withstand.

So, here America has an incredibly difficult decision. If it acts, there is no guarantee that democracy will take root in these developing countries. But doing nothing is no longer an acceptable solution. On the one hand, it might seem expedient to force the adoption of a constitution and a two-party voting system, but on the other hand, America does it with the knowledge that if the system is not accepted by the local people, it will be short-lived. All initial decisions needn't be made by the local populace. Part of the strategy must be to set up a referendum whereby the country's population could vote on the political and economic structures that are instituted. Their acceptance of any proposals through a nationwide referendum is an important step to ensure they are fully on board. For example, there should be a provision to separate church and state in any former Islamic dictatorship's new constitution but also a requirement that the general populace approve it by plebiscite. Human beings have to believe they are part of a process and embrace change of their own making before they are likely to accept it. If America's actions cannot pass this simple test, we will have replaced one dictatorship with another. And if the local people once freed from dictatorial coercion vote to rescind a new constitution or desire a religious autocracy, then so be it. The people have spoken. They may indeed learn from their neighbors who choose differently that there are alternative forms of government which will better provide for their well-being.

Obviously, there are large potential problems with this aggressive approach toward dictators. It will definitely add a level of instability to the world. The sovereignty of borders has allowed the modern world to settle into a relatively peaceful era of few wars and border disputes. By ending the sovereignty of select dictatorships, we run the risk of creating a period of country destabilization. Other countries, especially other dictatorships, will take this as an opportunity to attack neighbors preemptively. That is why it is so critical that any action on America's part have the blessing of an international body consisting of the democracies of the world.

There is another problem with having outsiders set up the government, political system, and economy for a developing country. If the world's experience with aid programs in the developing world has taught us anything, it is that programs that "provide" for the needs of a people run the risk of destroying the internal motivations of the people to care for themselves (Easterly, 2001). If a country's people feel they have others to look after them and control corruption and set up viable institutions, why would they do the hard work of actively participating in a democracy? If someone else is controlling your destiny, why would you pretend to be involved in self-governance? This is part of the problem with the World Bank's and the IMF's taking such a strong lead in the management of the economies of developing countries. Why would local citizens want to become involved in their government when all major decisions are being made by outsiders? The hardest part of initiating democracy overseas is to allow the citizens to make their own mistakes with a minimum of outside interference. Only through locally controlled democratic reform will citizens gain the authority to structure a government that is properly aligned with their dreams and ambitions. Then real economic development can occur. While painful to watch, we have to allow these fledgling new democracies to make their own mistakes. It's not as if we aren't making enough of our own back home in America.

9

WHAT SHOULD AMERICA'S MESSAGE TO THE DEVELOPING WORLD BE?

If local democracy and citizen participation are the keys to good government and a strong growing economy, how much involvement can America have in a developing country and not be disruptive to its citizens' attempts at self-rule? America sits on a vast reservoir of knowledge about what institutions are most helpful to stimulating growth in an economy. America ought to offer to share this knowledge but not make it a condition of aid and lending programs. The local people themselves have to decide what are appropriate government structures, constitutional guarantees, and human rights and educational initiatives. The United States has demonstrated time and again that it is not beyond making mistakes when offering

163

countries economic advice, including elevating American self-interests above the needs and desires of the local population. How do you find out these local needs? You ask! This is a rather radical approach given the arrogance with which America currently pursues its international relations.

Much of this book has been critical of the status quo. Here is an attempt to suggest advice for change that would bring immense good—nine steps to democratic freedom, individual liberty, and economic prosperity that America should promote to the developing world. These are only suggested steps; in each case, the country's people must decide for themselves whether they wish to enact them. Hopefully, those that decide to implement this plan will develop faster and become good role models for their neighbors who might be slower in adopting any change.

Step 1. Promote Law and Order

Afghanistan's weak federal government and its return to regional warlord dominance and poppy growing, Iraq's inability to police itself, and even Russia's unruly privatization scheme in the 1990s have vindicated those economists who preached how important a system of laws is to economic development. The world of economics had been kidnapped by free-market libertarians who thought that every situation could be made better if government involvement were reduced and regulation cut. They were guided by the fundamentally correct premise that private enterprise is almost always more efficient than government in providing goods and services to its citizens. What the traditional libertarians forgot was that basic fundamental economic exchanges in the private market sector required some degree of law and order to prevent coercion and fraud among participants and this is best provided by government.

Milton Friedman said it best when he was asked recently why he had recommended that the first three things Russia should do to grow faster in 1994 were "privatize, privatize, privatize." Friedman replied, "I was wrong, wrong, wrong!" Without proper rules in place to prevent securities fraud, stock manipulation, and outright theft and extortion, Russia's rush toward privatization led to nothing but the establishment of a corrupt layer of oligarchs who took over the private sector and ensured years of corruption to come.

To attain law and order, a society must meet a few prerequisites. First, It must have a body of law that is well thought out and defendable. Second, the judiciary must be independent (La Porta et. al., 1998). Many third-world countries pretend not to be dictatorships, but the leader always gets his way because he controls the judiciary. No official corruption is ever traced to his office because he controls the investigators, and a political opponent can be quickly squashed with false charges supported by crony judges.

The third component of an effective law and order system is not so obvious. Just as there are checks and balances on the legislative, executive, and judicial branches, so too must developing countries put checks on their enforcement staffs. A developing economy could quickly become a regulated police state if local magistrates enacted numerous regulations on the books and local police made a living taking bribes to look the other way. This is very common in the developing world and is one possible explanation for the plethora of regulations there (De Soto, 2000).

One possible solution to this problem, as it is to all problems of concentrated power, is to democratize. How do you spread the power of enforcement and policing to all the people so that it is more diluted, more democratic, less subject to abuse, and more in line with the people's wishes? One way is to have public- and private-sector whistle-blower statutes on the books in all city, state, and federal courts. Any citizen who found other citizens stealing, bribing, accepting bribes, extorting, or misusing their office and could prove the charge in a court of law would be eligible to receive 20% of any monies recovered, with no dollar maximum limit. To prevent a tag-team free-for-all from developing among the citizenry one could limit prosecution to offenders who were corporate officers of their companies or elected and appointed officials of government.

Law and order gains a negative connotation when it is used to mean forcefully quelling any dissent, especially when the poor working class has grievances with the rich. There is nothing to be gained economically or socially from suppressing the voice of the people violently, especially if their complaints have a basis in unjust wealth distribution or societal opportunities. Americans only have to remember the use of police dogs attacking citizens to quash the civil rights marches of the 1960s to realize how inappropriate such use of force under the banner of law and order is.

Step 2. Institute Land and Wealth Reform

It is quite ironic that to ensure democratic principles and respect for property rights take hold in a country, one of the initial steps might be to violate those very property rights. Many countries suffer de facto dictatorships because they have such a skewed distribution of wealth that it allows the elite to control the government. There are sham elections, but the wealthy decide whom each party nominates and how much money in support and advertising go to each candidate. Economists theorize that the presence of this wealthy controlling elite is what leads to corruption and influence peddling in government because the wealthy buy the legislation they want (Shleifer et al., 2003). Americans will recognize that such problems are not limited solely to the developing world.

Income and wealth distributions in the third world are typically far worse than in the wealthiest countries (Roll and Talbott, 2002). And in those democratic countries like Argentina and Brazil that still lag in development, it appears that it is their skewed income distribution that is preventing a broad-based recovery. In Argentina and Brazil, some 2% of the people own 98% of the land and natural resources.

It seems logical that if you want to encourage active citizenship in a democracy and a respect for property rights, you might want your citizenry to have some property to respect. An academic paper by Nancy Birdsall and Juan Luis Londono (1997) has demonstrated a tie between asset distribution and economic growth. The study found that countries with better asset distributions grew faster. Therefore, poor wealth distribution could delay growth, although the authors did not suggest a mechanism by which this occurs.

How is wealth reform accomplished? Different countries have done it differently. It does not necessarily have to involve a bloody revolution or class warfare. In America, Canada, and Australia, the frontier was opened and squatting laws allowed those who worked the land to acquire legal right to it (De Soto, 2000). It is my belief that broad land ownership served as a great impetus to the industrial revolution in these countries; a strong history of support for property rights was essential for the later development of rights to such intangibles as intellectual property and share ownership that became key ingredients in capitalism and industrialism.

In Japan after World War II, land reform was imposed on the citizenry as part of General Douglas MacArthur's occupation.

MacArthur wished to break up the power of the industrial cartels and large agricultural farmers, but he also understood the power of unleashing the working spirit of the Japanese laborers, including its women (Rajan and Zingales, 2003).

An excellent description of how wealth redistribution preceded democratic reform in early 18th and 19th century England can be found in Rajan and Zingales's book, *Saving Capitalism from the Capitalists*. The authors tell of the king who grabbed land from the church and distributed it to the lords and of the subsequent growth of the merchant class. With such broad distribution of land and resources, the king became reliant for his wealth on the lords' collection of taxes. Control slowly shifted from the king to the people, and eventually this relationship was cemented with the formation of Parliament and the end of the monarchy.

To show you the bias that many economists bring to a discussion of income redistribution, let me ask you how you would interpret the empirical finding that country incomes increase at the same time inequality of incomes declines (Roll and Talbott, 2002). A straightforward reading of this evidence would conclude that either better income distribution is good for growth or, somehow, richer countries become more egalitarian simply by becoming richer. For example, richer countries might be able to afford to implement more wealth transfer schemes such as welfare, Social Security, and Medicare.

How do many economists translate that same graphical picture of wealth increasing and inequality declining? In a rather convoluted argument, they give the following reason for the relationship: High levels of inequality impede growth because they motivate the disenfranchised poor to lobby their government for greater supposed antigrowth perks such as minimum wages, labor unions, and an increase in government spending programs. There is no evidence of such programs being antigrowth (Roll and Talbott, 2003). On the contrary, Roll and Talbott (Roll and Talbott, 2002) found that the wealthier countries of the world were more likely to have unions and that union participation was a significant variable that correlated highly with more egalitarian distributions of income.

Finally, some land and wealth reform can be relatively painless and not very revolutionary. Many governments have vast land holdings in the form of undeveloped land, national parks, military bases, palaces, and administrative office complexes. This land represents an excellent source of wealth and ownership that might be put to better use in the hands of the poor.

Step 3. Enact a Constitution and a Bill of Rights

Iraq is a wonderful test case for the most important reforms necessary to protect individual freedom and stimulate economic growth. As of the writing of this text, almost everyone involved in the reconstruction of Iraq is focusing on the introduction of the popular vote as the key pathway to freedom. The fact that many who were making this mistake were American is doubly painful, for it was the America's founders who were instrumental in writing one of the first constitutions that successfully preserved individual freedoms. The popular vote is incredibly important for liberty, but there can be no guarantees of individual liberties without a constitution and bill of rights (De Vanssay and Spindler, 1992).

Regardless of how a government is elected or formed, it must have sufficient power to prevent coercion of its citizens at the hands of any other country or group of citizens. A government must be strong enough to stand up to the ablest enemy abroad and the strongest consortium of corporations, workers, or citizens at home.

So the obvious question is how do you constrain the power of this expansive governmental entity you have created? You could trust the court systems and the judges to act responsibly in the future and always act in the people's interests. Or you could trust the president or Congress to always act in the people's interest. But what our country's founders intuitively knew from their experiences of living under an English monarch, no person could be assumed to use such powers responsibly. It is a lesson that many Americans today have forgotten. The founders chose to limit the powers of the government by a written document, the Constitution, and not leave the job to the whim of power-grabbing politicians of the future. More incredibly, after they devised this formula for controlling the government, they allowed their precious document to be subject to future amendment. Philosophically, they were saying that they thought they had the best solution, but if future generations wished to improve on their solution, that was fine.

So, back to Iraq. Here is a country that is approximately 62% Shiite Muslim, 35% Sunni Muslim, and 3% Christian (*CIA Factbook, 2003*). Religion is extremely important to all groups, and yet if a popular vote were installed, it is fairly likely an Islamic state led by the Shiites would be created. As soon as freedom was achieved, without constitutional guarantees concerning the practicing of religion, the basic right of approximately 40% of the country's people to practice their religion freely would be threatened. Even worse, all human rights would be threatened because religious law could be substituted for civil law making all decisions of the courts fairly arbitrary. There is no arguing with a religious court. Religious law is the first step to new dictatorship, as demonstrated in Iran.

Rights of minorities are poorly protected in popular-vote democracies. They are protected only by a constitution. It makes no sense to talk about individual freedom in Iraq until a constitution separating religion and state is ratified. And given the large percentage of Shiites in the country, any constitutional revisions might require 75% of the vote to further protect the individual rights of the religious minorities.

Is the U.S. Constitution with its Bill of Rights and subsequent amendments a good model for a developing country to use in building its own constitution? It is, with a few minor further amendments. The constitution is deficient in a few areas that the founding fathers could not possibly have predicted.

We should add an amendment to limit campaign contributions, prevent unlimited spending on campaign advertising, and fund some system of public campaign financing. Some would argue that this is a restriction of free speech. In a sense it is. That is why a constitutional amendment is necessary rather than just new legislation. Americans must consciously act to moderately limit free speech in order to preserve their democratic elections. There has to be a better understanding of freedom of speech versus allowing freedom of advertised or paid speech.

Also, to prevent incumbents from overtaking the government, there should be a constitutional limit on the terms any legislative representative could serve. Any problem associated with a lack of experience would be more than overly compensated with an elected body much more in tune with and responsive to the electorate. One should be very suspect of recent reports showing that term limits are ineffective and be sure to ask the basic question, is an incumbent or his representative the author of such a study.

There should also be real constraints on the government's ability to print money to fund its deficit positions. While troublesome in the developed countries and the leading cause of many of their recessions, this counterfeiting by a government can be devastating to a developing country. Many developing countries have to contend with inflation rates north of 20% per year, with some exceeding 100% per year. This makes normal operation of an economy almost impossible.

Lastly, constitutional limits on the size of government should be enacted. Government has to be strong, but not big. Limiting its size to 20% of total GDP seems reasonable, with possible limited short-term exceptions in time of war. There should also be a maximum borrowing allowable by the government, say, 50% of GDP. Again, such a provision would do more for the development of the private sector than all the lobbying efforts of all the corporations in the country.

So with a constitution that can effectively provide checks and balances on the government's power and guarantee individual liberties, a country is well poised to establish the kind of political and institutional environment to attract capital investment, encourage human capital development, and stimulate entrepreneurial activity necessary for a healthy and growing economy.

Step 4. Establish Strong Property Rights

Hernando de Soto (1989 and 2000) has written eloquently on the advantages to the poor in the developing world of their countries' adopting laws and customs that strongly support property rights. Not only are property rights the legal foundation for private property and capitalism, they also allow the poor the chance to develop their own homes and businesses without risk of having them expropriated by their government or by more sinister elements. But how can strong property rights systems be encouraged in developing countries in which many citizens hold little to no property? These growth initiatives should come from the general electorate, but what motivation does a landless population have in building a strong property rights system?

Is it hypocritical to take land from the wealthiest, distribute it to the poorest, and then turn around and talk about protecting private property? The key is understanding that ownership of property has moral standing only if one can defend the way the property was acquired and the effect the current wealth distribution has on the people's well-being. Just as a dictator has no moral authority to hold 98% of his country's assets while his citizens starve, so no small elite class can make a moral argument that it deserves 98% of the country's productive assets and land. The strongest argument it can make is that possession is nine-tenths of the law, but this carries little moral weight. Once a more equitable distribution of a country's assets that gives everybody in the country an opportunity to succeed has been achieved, property rights can be morally enforced. This distribution has the greatest chance of achieving the greatest good for all, and each individual is being treated fairly by the system.

Obviously, down the road, there will be disparities in incomes, but only if the distribution becomes so skewed as to represent a real threat to a fairness of opportunity should further redistributions be considered. The possibility of such potential additional redistributions should prevent the wealthy from seeking further gains when they already control most of the productive assets.

If this program of wealth redistribution sounds un-American to any wealthy Americans reading this book, consider the alternative. The wealthy could continue to grab an ever-increasing share of the wealth of the country until the people are fed up, at which point there probably won't be a country any more. Now that's un-American.

Step 5. Encourage Competitive Free Market Solutions to Public and Private Problems

Here is my *mea culpa* to the free market advocates I have abused in this treatise. Having spent far too much time on the free market's shortcomings, I now would like to insist that wherever possible and practical, the world look to the free market to solve its public- in addition to its private-sector problems.

First, this means that anything that can reasonably and fairly be accomplished by the private sector should be done there rather than being allocated to the government. Government is inefficient, not subject to a profit and loss system, and once it is involved in a business or activity, it is very hard to dislodge.

I hope that a new generation of economists would take it as a challenge to devise private solutions to public goods problems so that they could be provided by the private sector, addressing all the public's concerns without creating an unlimited profit-making opportunity. Trading markets in pollution rights and vouchers usable only in public schools are good examples of ways to bring market discipline to governmental allocation problems. Some regulation and oversight will be required but it will be better than giving the government carte blanche to do whatever they like.

Step 6. Constantly Review Government Regulations and Bureaucracy

What is it about the government bureaucracy that seems to make it continually grow and never shrink? Why is it that once government takes over a sector of the economy, it is very, very hard to make it relinquish it? Why does the number of regulations never diminish?

The primary problem with government regulation is that it has a very weak self-policing mechanism. Yes, democratic reforms can help, but elections every four years and journalistic exposes of abuse in the system are nowhere near as effective in improving efficiency as the competition inherent in a free market with immediate price movements, especially stock price movements. In private enterprise, suggestions that might lead to cost savings, streamlining, and increased profits are supposed to be welcomed by any employee. In a publicly run enterprise, opportunities for efficiency improvement scream out, and yet nothing is done. Why? What incentive do public workers have to work faster, smarter, or with fewer resources? All that can result is a need for fewer workers, which ultimately might threaten their jobs or put downward pressure on their wages.

There must be some way for real efficiency experts to be hired to review the operations of the government bureaucracy on a regular basis. They would have to be hired by an external party rather than as part of the bureaucracy itself. Their job would be not only to examine ways to work smarter and leaner but also to review the missions of various departments to see whether there is still a valid need for their services. It could bring a sense of strategic planning to government to structure public entities to provide the services they were initially charged with in a cost-efficient manner and move as many services as possible to the private sector. Getting this simple suggestion through a country's legislature would be no easy matter; government employees and departments are as an effective lobbying force as industry. Why do many governments seem to have too many employees? Because most government workers vote. Until citizens can get control of this very special special interest, world governments are doomed to ineffectiveness.

As discussed earlier, excessive regulation can be very debilitating to the formation of new business. While America is nowhere near as bureaucratic as, say, India, Peru, or Egypt, you have only to try to start a new business in America to see what a problem there is and feel utter sympathy for entrepreneurs in other countries of the world.

Why is excess regulation the norm around the world? Part of the problem is that once regulations are passed, they are hard to overturn. It is very easy for do-gooders to want to regulate a problem away and not do a good job of anticipating the ill-effects of excessive regulation. In effect, containing excessive regulation is itself a collective action problem that partially results from too many collective action problems being solved by regulation. Well-intentioned, concerned citizens may want to enact regulations to prohibit behavior they find offensive, but in so doing, they should weigh the fact that one more regulation adds to an already heavily regulated society in many countries.

So the problem in passing one more regulation is that it is costly to the person seeking individual liberty. It adds to the already burdensome collection of regulations one must live with. In the irony of ironies, good regulations are passed to solve collective action problems and increase human freedoms, and they instead overburden free-spirited individuals with excessive regulations, thus reducing their level of freedom. Think of John Wayne talking to an IRS representative and you will get the picture.

Regulations that are passed must be good regulations. Good regulations seem to be effective and efficient at solving a collective-action problem that could not be solved in the private marketplace, and beneficial enough for a majority of citizens to believe the new rules are worth having.

If this test were applied to current regulations, 90% of them might fail. Many existing regulations are ineffective and need review. In addition, many are written for situations that could be better solved with a change in individual motivations and incentives through free market principles than with the stick of increased regulation and enforcement.

The real reason behind much government regulation has not even been discussed. As George Stigler pointed out in his famous 1971 academic paper *Theory of Economic Regulation,* much government regulation is in place because the industry or enterprise being regulated wants it there. This seems almost counterintuitive at first. Why would industry want itself regulated?

It is true that most regulation is initiated by well-meaning souls who are concerned with a particular problem and wish government to intervene. But it is also the nature of economics and politics that long after these well-meaning individuals and groups lose interest in the cause or lose their funding, the regulations they initiated are still on the books and new regulatory bodies with great power have been created to oversee an industry or an issue. At this time, industry uses its economic and political weight to co-opt the mission of the regulatory agency and even rewrite the regulations in many cases so that they are much more favorable to industry. In fact, they turn out not only to be less onerous than they were originally, but they benefit industry. How could this be?

Primarily, the regulatory bodies are used by incumbent industry participants to exclude new entrants to the business. They can do this through tariffs and quotas to keep out foreign competition or through operating requirements that only existing businesses can satisfy. Bidding requirements can be built into government contracts such that only incumbents qualify. Regulations allowing industry participants to preserve local monopolies also greatly benefit their profitability. Price supports and subsidies are also greatly appreciated by incumbent business. Finally, requiring licenses for occupations such as barbers, beauticians, tanning salon operators, and veterinarians probably adds little value to their services, but it acts to protect the salaries of these professionals from other labor competition. Stigler examines the positive impact regulation had on the profits of the trucking industry in the 1960s, but his examples could easily be updated to the present through a review of recent regulations' positive impact on the profits of the cable television business, the banking and brokerage industries, HMOs, or tobacco companies.

Given the large amount of fairly useless regulation in the world, some of it is probably performing a service for some incumbent politicians and businesspeople. The most devastating effect of onerous regulation in a developing country is that it prevents a poor, but motivated, person from seeking employment or starting a business. It would be logical to assume that this barrier was not constructed unintentionally but was built in cooperation by the incumbent government and private market workers who see the unemployed and uneducated as the greatest threat to their livelihoods. In many countries, the number of people working in the informal sector, or black market, can exceed 40% of the working age population (De Soto, 1989 and 2000). What better way to protect incumbent jobs and wages than to increase regulation to the point that others decide entering the formal sector just isn't worth it?

Now having spent a great deal of time warning about the dangers of too much meaningless regulation, I acknowledge that some regulation is necessary and desirable for the following reasons:

- The rules of the game must be clearly specified to encourage active economic participants to invest time and money.

- Rules must establish systems of fairness and justice so that everyone buys into the system.

- To ensure transparency and fairness, market participants must use proper accounting and management.

- Some governments can make great strides in providing public goods and solving collective action problems by making wise use of regulations that most of the citizens want.

Let's be certain industry doesn't throw out necessary regulation when the people make an assault on excessive and burdensome regulation.

Step 7. Establish a Free Press

People often underestimate the importance of a free press to democracy. As mentioned previously, it is just now becoming understood how important a contribution a truly independent news media makes to economic growth and prosperity (Roll and Talbott, 2003). Therefore, a country must look at its news and media operations as more than just another industry.

We saw earlier that in order for democracy to work and aid in the development of a healthy economy, the elected leaders and representatives need feedback from their citizens. This can come from elections held once every four years, but effective feedback must come more frequently. One solution would be for all citizens of the country to monitor the government every day—interesting but not very efficient. The news media is an alternative solution. The media is in effect the people's hired gun. People buy their papers and watch their commercials, but in return, they ask the media to monitor the operations of their government and the largest corporations on an almost daily basis.

When the media is effective in acting as this monitor of the government, it is honest, unbiased, timely, and informative. When the media becomes solely a for-profit business, its objectives change to become entertaining, attractive, interesting, and profitable. This is a classic case of poor alignment of goals and objectives. What for-profit media outlet would blow the whistle on its own corporate parent, or the media industry for that matter, or any business trying to grab tax breaks? As a matter of fact, why would any for-profit news outlet seek out and report corruption of any governmental or business executive? At best, it might get a short-term ratings boost, but it might be blacklisted by other bigwigs who refuse to appear on their program in the future.

Why would a country's media do any in-depth study of a real problem facing the country? It would be too long and too boring and have too many talking heads. The average attention span of the audience is too short.

I believe for a news media to be unbiased, it must be publicly owned. Not that the business could not employ private market-type incentives, but these motivators should be tied to the goals of a responsible media and not to increasing ratings and profits. There is a very real likelihood that if democracy dies, the infestation will have attacked its for-profit media first. There is nothing wrong with having private news media companies also to assure a degree of competition and prevent the government from monopolizing the news, but every country as a prerequisite of maintaining its democratic freedom should have a well financed public news media outlet.

Step 8. Institute Civil Liberties

It is historically interesting that the founders of our country forgot to include the specific protections of individual rights and liberties called the Bill of Rights in their original Constitution. Given their recent repressive experience with a ruling British monarch and the revolution they had just fought, the importance of these individual liberties may have been assumed by all present. But the Bill of Rights and accompanying Amendments give a wonderful delineation of just how powerful those individual rights and liberties are.

Any developing country would be wise to also delineate in constitutional form the specific rights enjoyed by every one of its citizens. Are we talking about men, women, elder people, younger people, endangered species? And what rights will you give these participants? The right to bear arms? The right to peacefully assemble? To choose their religion? To protest? To enjoy fair and accurate reporting by their government and their industries? To have equal representation in their government? To exclude corporations from the political process?

Each country will develop a different bill of rights. While Americans rightfully trust and respect their constitutional formation, each developing country should be left free to develop its own system of protecting the rights it feels are most important to its own citizens.

Step 9. Establish the Popular Vote

When people think of establishing a democracy, the popular vote is what they typically think of. Would it surprise you to know that solely from an economic perspective, this is not the most important step? In getting an economy growing, it is more important to introduce economic freedoms such as the rule of law and property rights. What good is the vote if the economy continues to decline? How long do you think your narrow definition of democracy would survive?

Our research (Roll and Talbott 2003) also showed that establishing civil liberties and a free press were, statistically speaking, even more important to economic prosperity than was establishing a popular vote. While it is possible to have meaningful growth in a benevolent dictatorship such as Hong Kong under the British (no vote, but free press and civil liberties), the only way to ensure that leaders maintain their benevolence is to abide by the vote. The rule of law, property rights, and civil liberties are all important for economic development—but the only way to be sure a government will enact them, protect them, and maintain them is by having a popular vote. It is the ultimate in self-policing mechanisms for governments, and as the failure of world aid organizations has shown, if you do not police your own government, no one else is capable of doing it for you.

Who Will Tell
the People?

All the ills of democracy can be cured by more democracy.
ALFRED EMANUEL SMITH

10

HAS ACADEMIA LOST ITS INDEPENDENCE?

If you agree that the story told so far in this text is an extremely important and disturbing one, you might ask why it wasn't exposed sooner. The American government depends on a two-party system in which each party should be anxious to expose bad behavior on the part of the other. Unfortunately, both parties are feeding from the same trough. Their candidates depend on corporate and special-interest monies to help them get reelected. One can't expect an incumbent to rat on another incumbent because they both are benefiting enormously from the system.

There is a far wider story of influence and power, far beyond the halls of Congress. It would not be sufficient for the most powerful in our country to be able to try to influence the government unfairly if the country's media or academia could easily blow the whistle on this abuse of democracy.

But how could corporations and the wealthy have acted to prevent the media or academia from playing their roles as watchdogs to our democracy? One might assume there was some sort of secret conspiracy in which corporations quietly overtook our colleges and our news media. Here, however, activities were much more out in the open. You don't have to believe in secret initiation rituals at the Skull and Bones Society at Yale, strange Masonic meetings held in the dead of night, a Trilateral Commission, or even a New World Order to understand how big corporations and the wealthy were able to organize their efforts effectively to corrupt our government and influence our media and our academics. The Republican Party was the primary engine behind this movement, but many smaller conservative groups interested in further enrichment of American corporations and its wealthiest also took part.

To demonstrate how publicly these actions occurred, at least monthly for the last 10 years, Alan Greenspan, the chairman of the Federal Reserve Board, has announced in a press release that he was fighting the reoccurrence of inflation by successfully preventing wages from rising. Whose wages did you think he has been talking about? He is speaking on behalf of the investor and corporate elite of this country who see higher wages as a problem that restricts corporate profits. Why would middle-class workers ever vote Republican?

Universities, first and foremost, should be centers of learning and the acquisition of knowledge. History has taught us that both teaching and learning proceed best when the environment is free of bias and prejudice. Every university should be a free marketplace of ideas. Free speech rights are of the utmost importance everywhere in a democracy, but probably nowhere are they as important as on a university campus. University professors and students must feel free to express their ideas if true learning is to occur. It is in the very nature of the evolution of knowledge that arguments are required to hash out new ideas, that these new ideas must replace the old, and such regeneration is inhibited if there is a bias toward a particular approach or belief, especially the status quo.

Universities, in addition to providing a haven for the discussion of new and often times unpopular ideas, have a very important role to play in a well-functioning democracy. Academics occupy an important place in society because they are regarded as intelligent, knowledgeable, expert, and generally unbiased. (The fact that academics themselves realize this makes it sometimes difficult for them to embrace the democratic idea that everyone's vote should be treated equally. Sometimes, because of their own great personal investment in knowledge, they are slow to understand the reasoning of a democracy that says every person's vote should be equal. In a sense, this makes them intellectual elites and as such they have to be sure they don't inhibit democratic reforms in order to protect their privileged positions.) This highly regarded status is conferred by society because citizens believe that academics work very hard for less than they might earn in the real world—and historically have worked hard to preserve their intellectual independence. Their independent status, unbiased perspective, and huge reservoir of intellect and knowledge lead professors often to be called as expert witnesses in court trials and are the reason their letters to the editors of America's newspapers carry such weight. Citizens, and courts, trust and respect their views because they presume those views to be independently generated, to speak for the public good, and not to have any secret or undisclosed other interest or master to serve.

Because Americans believe them to be unbiased, they often turn to their universities when confronting dilemmas facing the republic and their beloved democracy. They assume an academic will arrive at a fair solution, having no axe to grind. And academics have often played important roles as fact checkers and overseers of the operations of the government and the business community. The antiwar protest movement during the Vietnam conflict is but one example of a moral initiative that started on college campuses across the country. Much of the support for the civil rights movement, the women's movement, and the attack on global sweatshops can be traced back to campuses. If universities were to lose their unbiased moral compass, the loss would be felt by not only students but by the total democracy. Unions, churches, and the media also try to play this oversight role to some degree, but they all carry with them particular ingrained biases that make their roles more suspect.

It is probably fair to say that most universities historically have had a liberal bias. But in the last 30 years, this has begun to change. Although there are still many liberals on college campuses, there is a new breed of professor who is much more comfortable with, and closer to, business and industry. Many reside in the nation's business schools, who at least practice full disclosure in identifying themselves as associated with a "business" school. Being pro-business is not necessarily a bad thing—only when it gets in the way of a professor's ability to think freely and speak freely should alarms sound. A professor's particular belief system is his own business, but when industry interferes on campus to try to sway professors' opinions and views with dollars and prestigious opportunities and assignments then one should be concerned.

The most important task most university presidents have on campus today is not recruiting excellent students or professors but raising money for the university's endowment. Even many state-supported schools have moved to an endowment structure to assist in filling the gaps left by government funding cutbacks. Therefore, successful university presidents today are more likely to be those with strong business and investment skills and good relationships with the business community.

Where does the money come from to fund an endowment? If it is not coming directly from a corporation or a corporate foundation, it is most likely coming from an alumnus who works or worked at a corporation. In today's world, corporations and their executives control most of the purse strings on campus. You can see the danger. It is very important to know what promises a university is making to attract this corporate largesse. If capital contributed to the school has contingencies attached to it, it can make the independent running of the school difficult, if not impossible. Once the school accepts monies from a corporate donor and applies them toward the school's operating budget, that donor has incredible leverage over how that school acts in the future. There is no law against a corporate donor's making demands in exchange for funding, but it can weaken the independence that every school desires and craves.

Lawrence Soley, in his book *Leasing the Ivory Tower: The Corporate Takeover of Academia,* gives a rather minor example of Glassboro State College, which accepted a $100 million gift from Henry M. Rowan in 1992. Part of the money was to be used for student scholarships for children of Rowan's company's employees, but only non-union employees. Given the magnitude of the total gift, Glassboro State College officials decided initially to accept this discriminatory condition, but union and media pressure eventually forced Rowan to reverse his original position and allow the funds to be used for all employees' children. Is it not amazing how fuzzy our logic becomes when someone dangles $100 million dollars in front of us?

In a more prominent case, in 2000, Phil Knight, the CEO of Nike, Inc., announced he was withdrawing his commitment to give

$30 million to the University of Oregon, his alma mater. He was upset because, against his urging, the university had decided to join the Worker Rights Consortium (WRC). This organization looks into the unfair treatment of workers in sweatshops around the world, primarily in the footwear and apparel industries. Not by coincidence, these are the two largest business sectors for Knight's firm. (*U.S. News and World Report*, 5/15/00).

The University's action had the full support of students and faculty. It was an incredibly important issue to the students because surveys had shown that much of the apparel and footwear produced in these sweatshops was being sold on college campuses, often at school-sponsored bookstores. Here was an ideal opportunity for students to feel some sense of solidarity and compassion with workers halfway around the world who seemed to need their assistance. Besides teaching important participatory democratic principles, what university would not be proud if it could teach its students the simple lesson of human compassion?

In time, Knight became a financial supporter of the school's football team again, but not before the Oregon's Board of Higher Education ruled that the university could not join an organization such as the WRC. Supposedly, the reason Knight reversed his decision never to support the school again was not a plea from the president or the dean of students, but a threat from the football coach to move to Ohio State unless Knight resumed his financial support.

In an even more disturbing trend, corporate contributions and monies are finding their way directly onto campuses. For a reasonable price, a corporate or wealthy private donor can fund a named academic chair, a department, a new wing, a building, a stadium, or an entire school. It must be hard to have to try to conduct unbiased research with a corporate name, the name of a Wall Street titan, or an industry's moniker on a professor's business card. Try acting and teaching without bias when your official title is, "The K-Mart Professor of Marketing and Business Strategy". Professors would only be acting rationally if they began to ease up on any work critical of either business in general or the industry or company funding their chairs. In a world where Americans are concerned when their city's stadium is renamed after a corporation, why is there no outrage when their institutions of higher learning are sold to the highest bidder? Americans shouldn't care much if Michael Jordan has been bought by Nike, but they should definitely care if Nike has purchased their academic elite.

Professors' relationships with corporate America are not limited to the partial funding of their salaries. Many professors make multiples of their base salaries from consulting relationships they have in the private sector. A general rule on most campuses is that professors can spend 20% of their work time on these consulting assignments, supposedly because spending time in the real world keeps the academic current. The problem is that professors so dependent on consulting gigs will be very slow to say or write anything critical of business. Active academic consultants become very friendly with their corporate hosts who often fund expensive trips to faraway conferences and even act as sources of funding for academic publication needs.

A specific type of consulting that academics provide is in giving expert testimony at trials. Even if academics act completely ethically in arriving at their expert advice, they may be very unlikely to risk this income stream by doing or saying anything against corporate entities because big corporations make the best repeat clients. Some of these experts are paid tens of thousands of dollars per day for their testimony. There is great pressure to have the testimony come out the way one's employer wishes it to. It is not proper to assign blame to all members of academia, but one only has to observe professors giving expert testimony funded by the tobacco industry that tobacco products are not addictive to see there is a real problem.

In addition to consulting practices, many professors in medicine, biology, physics, business, and computer science have established their own businesses, often in partnership with corporate America. The innovations and research that many academics are in the business of generating are easily turned into profit-making patentable businesses. In partnership with biotech, computer chip, pharmaceutical, brokerage, and defense companies, these small jointly owned companies have enormous upside potential. While it is wonderful to see academics benefiting from their inventions, this kind of activity reinforces the bonds between academia and business and further invites conflicts of interest and bias onto campus. As my professor friend told me, "Isn't the first job of a university professor to teach?". Professors can easily move into the private sector if their primary interest is research or business.

Campus environments themselves have changed tremendously over the years. Students now receive fellowships funded by corporations, sometimes based on how well they embody the ideal corporate cog. There are research paper contests that reward the students best at explaining the beauties of the free market system. You can assume that a student who submitted a paper extolling the necessity of government regulation would be about as welcome as that high schooler who showed up in Atlanta on his school's Coca-Cola day wearing a Pepsi tee-shirt. Students on campus no longer wear hats with the nickname of the football team on them, but instead wear shoes with the Nike swoosh, sweatshirts with Abercrombie and Fitch emblazoned on them, and baseball caps with Adidas stitched across the brow. The cafeteria food is just as unhealthy as it always was, but now it comes in wrappers that say Burger King or McDonalds. Your university is either a Coke or Pepsi franchise, and your entire athletic department is a Nike or Adidas franchise because the company gave your school tens of millions of dollars for the exclusive rights to your campus and agreed to outfit your sports teams and fund their activities. The football stadium has a corporate name on it, as does the bowl game your team goes to.

Table 10.1 lists the college football bowl game lineup for 2003/ 2004. If the Humanitarian Bowl, the only bowl game on the list not named after a corporate sponsor, lived up to its name, it would

Table 10.1 College Football Bowl Games, 2003/2004

GAME	TEAMS	DATE
GMAC Bowl	Miami (Ohio) vs. Louisville	December 18
Mazda Tangerine Bowl	NC State vs. Kansas	December 22
Sheraton Hawaii Bowl	Houston vs. Hawaii	December 25
Insight Bowl	California vs. Virginia Tech	December 26
Continental Tire Bowl	Pittsburgh vs. Virginia	December 27
MasterCard Alamo Bowl	Michigan State vs. Nebraska	December 29
EV1.net Houston Bowl	Navy vs. Texas Tech	December 30
Pacific Life Holiday Bowl	Washington State vs. Texas	December 30
Gaylord Hotels Music City Bowl	Wisconsin vs. Auburn	December 31
Wells Fargo Sun Bowl	Minnesota vs. Oregon	December 31
AXA Liberty Bowl	Southern Miss vs. Utah	December 31
Diamond Walnut Bowl	Colorado State vs. Boston College	December 31
Outback Bowl	Iowa vs. Florida	January 1
Toyota Gator Bowl	West Virginia vs. Maryland	January 1
Capital One Bowl	Purdue vs. Georgia	January 1
Rose Bowl, presented by Citi	USC vs. Michigan	January 1
FedEx Orange Bowl	Miami vs. Florida State	January 1
SBC Cotton Bowl	Oklahoma State vs. Mississippi	January 2
Chick-fil-A Peach Bowl	Clemson vs. Tennessee	January 2
Tostitos Fiesta Bowl	Kansas State vs. Ohio State	January 2
Humanitarian Bowl	Georgia Tech vs. Tulsa	January 3
Nokia Sugar Bowl	Oklahoma vs. LSU	January 4

Source: www.espn.go.com

pass out handguns at halftime so the fans could put themselves out of their misery at having to endure this sell-out to big business.

In one of the more disturbing corporate invasions on campus, commercial banks and credit card companies are actively marketing credit cards to students. The marketing efforts are endorsed by the university that often grants an exclusive relationship to one credit card vendor. Such an exclusive relationship results in a credit card with the university's logo proudly displayed in exchange for access to student, university employee and alumni mailing lists.

The principle behind credit cards is that the borrower has some means of income to pay off the balance. Students, by definition, do not. A part-time job at minimum wage is not sufficient to pay back allowable balances, especially when the student is in the middle of an extremely expensive academic undertaking. Credit card companies often get students to overconsume, overborrow, and then under great debt burdens, rely on their parents to straighten out their accounts. Parents are told that unless they pay up, the kid's credit rating will be damaged forever, making getting a job extremely difficult (*Money,* September 1994). A cynic would think that this is the *modus operandi* of these banks from the start. For the grief it causes the overleveraged students and for the problems it presents in repaying the loan upon graduation, it just isn't worth it. Unfortunately, many students today graduate with enough student loans, car loans and credit card debt that they never have any choice but to buy into the system and take an entry-level job in corporate America. A $22,000-a-year job working for a non-profit organization wouldn't generate enough money to repay these loans, much less start one on buying a home at today's prices. So by inviting credit card companies onto college campuses, school administrators are damaging the independence of the next generation. It is not long after graduation that these students, comfortable with excessive leverage, sign their first home mortgage and effectively complete the sale of their facility for independent and critical thinking in the never-ending pursuit of keeping up with their neighbors.

The economics and business course curriculum on campus is clearly bent toward free market economics, and very little is said against business in class. It is hard to find any course critical of capitalism in a typical college curriculum guide. Any discussion of the possible ill effects of globalization on developing countries will most likely be heard on the commons rather than in the classroom. Any suggestion that the labor market is not a perfect market and might need intervention by government or unions to ensure fairness is met with wide-eyed stares of disbelief from the faculty.

One of the findings of the Roll/Talbott (2003) academic research was that international trade levels (measured as a percentage of GDP) had zero effect on a country's personal incomes. How could such an obvious and important result go unreported to date? Hundreds of research papers in economics have examined the relationship between trade and country economic growth and they have always concluded a favorable and positive relationship existed between the two. Even empirical research papers that find no statistical relationship between trade and growth couch their results by concluding in their summaries that no new evidence was found in their studies that would refute the belief that trade aids growth. This is like saying that after examining the correlation of donut sales and subsequent police activity in cities there is no new evidence in conflict with the theory that the sun doesn't rise in the West and set in the East. Is it a coincidence that America's biggest companies insist that there is free trade in order to expand their markets? If you understand this one example, you can see the real difficulty in having academia lose its independent perspective. Based on possible faulty and biased research, the developing countries of the world may spend decades trying to export their way to prosperity. What seems like a small problem on university campuses has very far-reaching, and costly, implications.

In addition to teaching, universities act as the primary facility for conducting long-term research in America. Although it is helpful to have relationships with industry to ensure that this research has some practicality, society pays a high price if these relationships are too close. First, industry is not interested in very long-term research for research's sake. Corporations want earnings, and preferably in the next quarter. And yet it is exactly this kind of long-term research that incubates entire new processes, products, companies, and industries. Second, and not surprisingly, published research funded by a particular industry is rarely, if ever, critical of that industry. While most professors are ethically above actually changing the results of an experiment to support a sponsor, it is amazing how powerful self-deception is when the results are interpreted. People see what they want to see.

Just as disturbing is the practice of not publishing results that either refute or fail to support a sponsor's position. It is easy for many researchers to either redo the experiment or make subtle changes until they achieve more sponsor-friendly results. Most troublesome are contractual agreements with the sponsor that prevent releasing data without their approval—a condition that ensures only pro-sponsor evidence will ever be released publicly. Finally, how could researchers not feel an ethical obligation to disclose the source of their funding if it is material to the research? Wouldn't people want to know that research conducted to measure the harmful effects of smoking was being funded by Phillip Morris?

Lawrence Solely reports that the amount of corporate research money going to universities increased fivefold during the 1980s. He cites a rather egregious example of corporate access and influence at MIT. There, professors earn "bonus points" if they are supportive of the school's efforts to attract corporate involvement on campus.

Professors get one point for providing an unpublished research paper to a corporation, two points for a corporate phone conversation, and 12 points for a visit to a corporate headquarters. Each point can be redeemed for prizes and each is worth approximately $35. Unfortunately, no points are given for showing up to class on time, updating last year's notes before giving a lecture, telling a great joke in class, scheduling office time to speak to students, or writing a piece of research that truly revolutionizes the way people think about their place in the world. Thankfully, many such points-based incentive award programs have found to be rather ineffective in changing long-term human behavior.

The impact of corporate influence on campuses appears to be growing. It has affected the curriculum of the schools, lessened the importance of teaching as research has become more highly emphasized, reduced academic freedom, strained professorial ethics, and damaged the sterling reputations of some of the country's finest institutions of higher learning. Derek Bok, the former president of Harvard, provides further testimony to the ever-increasing commercialization of our university campuses in his excellent text, *Universities in the Marketplace : The Commercialization of Higher Education* (Bok 2003).

The influence of corporations on college campuses is not so pervasive that it has completely changed the culture of America's universities. But for it to do damage to America's democracy, it does not have to be ubiquitous. It need only establish a foothold such that one or two professors can conduct phony favorable research, give supportive, but false, expert testimony, and write enthusiastic op-ed pieces sympathetic to the company's causes without being shut down by the administration. If this is allowed to happen, a few bad professors will have cashed in on and destroyed an academic reputation that took generations to build. One or two bad apples can most definitely spoil the bunch. The problem with impeccable reputations is they can easily be destroyed even if the vast majority of academia continues to honor their oaths by performing to the highest ethical standards. If a few damage the sanctity of academia, then all who did not act early to straighten out this problem will have to share in the blame.

Historically, citizens turned to university professors for an educated and unbiased opinion about the effects of new governmental laws and regulations and for their views on new political and economic agendas. The universities now have competition. The last 30 years has seen an explosion of think tanks, located both on and off college campuses. Most of these institutions are conservative, and the most popular causes they fight for are tax relief, free markets, and a strong defense establishment.

To call think tanks research institutes is a misnomer. These institutions get almost all of their financial backing from wealthy conservative individuals and corporations. There was never a piece of "research" that these institutions completed that did not support their basic philosophy. This either is the luckiest streak of experiments in history, all providing supporting evidence that their organization's philosophy is universally correct—which is very unlikely—or offers proof that their research and reporting are extremely biased. Could you imagine working at a privately funded think tank and trying to publish an article directly contradicting the philosophy of your boss, your company, its founders, and its financial backers? You would not only lose face, you would probably lose the job that goes along with that face. This demonstrates how important academic freedom is at our universities. If professors detect even a hint of an administration bias, their self-deception will work overtime to achieve an intellectual position that guarantees their job preservation.

The biggest off-campus conservative think tanks are the American Enterprise Institute (AEI), the Heritage Foundation, the Center for Strategic and International Studies (CSIS), and the Cato Institute, all conveniently headquartered in Washington (*The Nation,* 12/22/97). It is convenient because it is not research but lobbying that these institutions are in the business of. The employees of these think tanks are often called "scholars" in an attempt to polish their reputations, but many are either unemployed lobbyists or ex-government employees. To make their work appear more scholarly, the think tanks have started their own "research" journals, although there is little to no peer review required to have an article published. The AEI's journal, *Public Opinion,* and the Heritage Foundation's *Policy Review* may sound just academic enough to fool the general public. University professors lend their institutions' reputations to these phony journals by agreeing to write articles for them, for a fee of course.

Conservative think tanks have discovered that dollars equals research. As long as you don't feel compelled to report all your results, you can continue to conduct experiments and basic research until you find support for your philosophy—that is, as long as you are well funded. Not only do increased dollars create the potential for false research, but a well-funded marketing machine can see to it that your phony research will be in the hands of every congressional representative and on the nightly news while the theoretically correct research of the opposition languishes in the back of a less-well-financed, but real, academic research journal in the campus library.

So the wealthy and the corporations are creating their own scientific evidence and building their own "academic" institutions to buttress their worldview. Is it a coincidence that these think tanks' worldview of free markets, lower taxes, and bigger defense spending agrees with that of their corporate financial backers? Would a research institute conclude it is appropriate to cut defense spending when that same research institute is funded by defense contractors?

There ought to be a law. Such fraudulent lobbying of Congress ought to carry the same penalties as false advertising for consumer products. People ought to feel free to creatively construct and publish whatever phony "scientific" evidence they wish to present to their government representatives as long as they don't mind spending the next 10 years of their life in solitary confinement writing research articles solely for the prison journal.

And so, corporations and the wealthy have a much greater say on our college campuses and in our think tanks than years before. While opening up many avenues of enriching our elite academics, we should remain cautious that we do not lose the freedoms on campus that are so important not only for the education of our children but the preservation of our democracy. Like all long–term strategic issues, the true pain will not be felt by Americans until it is too late to act.

11

WHO CONTROLS THE MEDIA?

The current great debate in media circles is whether the media in America has a liberal or a conservative bias. Some statistics say that 90% of on-air television news reporters vote Democratic. In addition, a number of best-selling books recently purport to expose this supposed liberal bias (see *The Savage Nation: Saving America from the Liberal Assault on Our Borders, Language, and Culture* by Michael Savage and *Bias: A CBS Insider Exposes How the Media Distort the News* by Bernard Goldberg).

At one time, most of the newspapers, radio stations, and television networks in our country were owned by individuals, many potentially with a liberal bias. Their journalists grew up recognizing the critical importance that the media plays in acting as a watchdog of our government and the largest corporations in the country, and they took great pride in confronting the establishment when good journalism dictated that they must.

There has been a tremendous sea of change in the last 30 years in the make-up of the media. Almost all areas of the media industry have become dominated by corporations, and mostly by very large media conglomerates. Robert W. McChesney has documented these changes in his excellent book, *Rich Media, Poor Democracy* to demonstrate how dramatic and far reaching this consolidation has been.

McChesney names five conglomerates that dominate the media landscape:

- AOL/Time Warner (WB)

- Disney (ABC)

- Viacom (CBS)

- Rupert Murdoch's News Corporation (Fox)

- Sony

They own and operate businesses in almost every arena of media, and as McChesney points out, they are eager to make bigger inroads into non-media businesses with product tie-ins and merchandise promotions. They own national television networks, television production facilities, television stations in local markets, cable TV programming and channels, newspapers, magazines, book publishers, radio stations, music businesses, and movie studios and movie distribution businesses. And that is just in the U.S. They are very aggressively adding to their empires internationally. Right behind them are General Electric, which owns NBC, and AT&T, which purchased TCI, the largest cable TV business in the country.

As McChesney demonstrates, corporate ownership and consolidation in each of the media business segments has grown tremendously. Television is dominated by the four networks—ABC, NBC, CBS, and Fox—that are now all owned by very large corporations. News Corp. and its network, Fox, both are controlled by Rupert Murdoch, one of the most conservative businessmen in the world. In cable TV, seven firms control 75% of all cable channels and programming. In radio, traditionally a local medium, four giants control one-third of the total industry revenue of $13.6 billion, and much of the programming is produced nationally. Independent newspapers have been bought up by six major chains led by Gannett, Knight-Ridder, The Tribune Company, and The New York Times Company. Hundreds of previously independent book publishers have been swallowed by seven dominant firms, while 80% of all books sold in the U.S. are retailed through a handful of national chains including Amazon.com, Borders and Barnes & Noble. The six largest film studios distribute 90% of all U.S. movies. Since Seagram purchased Polygram, the five largest music companies control 87% of the domestic music business. The jury is still out on attempts to concentrate ownership among Internet businesses, but each of the major conglomerates has made moves to try to wrest some control over what is presented as a rather uncontrollable medium. Time Warner merged with Internet giant AOL.

In 2003, the Federal Communications Commission (FCC) tried to allow further consolidation in television by allowing TV networks to own stations covering up to 45% of the total U.S. audience. The previous limit was 35% (*Business Week*, 9/22/03). In what many viewed as a healthy reawakening of democratic outrage by the American people, the House voted 400 to 21 to overturn the new FCC regulations, followed by a similar 55 to 40 vote in the Senate. But were these actions inspired by a great groundswell of protest by the American people that finally caused their representatives in Washington to act in a true democratic spirit or were there other more sinister forces at work? (*The New York Times,* 11/21/03).

During the House debate on the new FCC regulations, House Speaker Dennis Hassert, Republican of Illinois, fought to keep the issue from debate and vote on the floor, and the Bush administration threatened a veto if the FCC regulations were overturned (*Television Week,* 11/10/03). It turns out that the real battle lines may not have been between the public and the networks at all but rather between the networks and their station affiliates who felt threatened by the regulations. The revocation in the Congress may have had more to do with the representatives' dependence on these local stations for campaign ad time than any great groundswell of the American people. CBS, NBC, and Fox have petitioned a federal court arguing that limiting their signal to "only 45% of households deprives them of their right of free speech in the other 55% of households" (*Multichannel News,* 11/10/03). In essence, they are arguing that their right to free speech allows them the opportunity to create a monopoly of not "free" but "paid-for" speech.

While most people in the debate focused on the 45% limit on television station ownership, which was subsequently repealed by Congress, other important provisions of the new FCC regulations sailed through untouched. These would allow companies to snap up not only two to three local TV stations in a market but also a newspaper and up to eight radio stations (*Business Week,* 9/22/03). Such local media concentration could create localized media monopolies, not only on profits but also on the way Americans receive their news.

How is America's democracy threatened if media outlets are owned by a few, well-connected media conglomerates? Although the fact that all movies, music, and entertainment programming are created and distributed by a few well-heeled corporations should give one pause, it is the collection and distribution of news that most affects a democracy. One could easily argue that our culture is as threatened as our democracy by the concentration of so many important art forms in a few corporate hands, but that is outside the purview of this book. In the long-term, a corporate takeover of our most important music, film and culture could represent just as serious threat to our democracy as much of our free speech is represented in our arts and entertainment.

Immediate threats to our democracy are the primary concern here, and a fundamental requirement of any democracy is easy access to current and unbiased news. News about the country's government and how it is performing is critical, but also important is news about competing political parties, America's largest corporations, the way the outside world views America and its leaders, and general reports about the welfare of the American people and their needs and desires. If the citizenry is unable to obtain such unbiased reporting in a timely fashion, people cannot be expected to be able to effectively judge the performance of their leaders or to monitor them properly. Any feedback the public gives its leaders is only as good as the information the public is given to react to.

So in this regard, a corporate roundup of the media businesses is most damaging if it adds a bias to the reporting of news in the country. As mentioned earlier, many people who enter the news profession, at least historically, may have had a somewhat liberal bias. The grand ambition of a great journalist, to find an earth-shattering story that exposes corruption or fraud at the highest levels of government or industry, fits a renegade-type, non-establishment personality. But is this the kind of person the corporate media is hiring today? Are media outlets trying to find tough investigative journalists? Are they looking for the next Mike Wallace? No, many of the news anchors today are simply reading the evening news off cue cards, which is a far cry from the leadership roles Walter Cronkite and Edward R. Murrow played at CBS. The ideal hire at a network today is someone who will take orders from corporate headquarters and toe the line.

And what of these supposedly liberal news people who currently inhabit the terrain? If you saw any of the coverage of the latest war against Iraq, you would think they had lost whatever liberal bias they might have had. They were openly cheering the U.S. troops, many of them for good reason since they were embedded with the troops and their lives depended on them. What a great way to get the media to be more pro-military—put them on the front lines. That will get them supporting increased military budgets in the future. When your life depends on the soldiers around you, you gain a whole new appreciation for their importance.

Andrew Tyndall, an independent news analyst, says the television news media covered the buildup to war with the majority of the reporting originating from the White House, Pentagon, and State Department while it ignored smaller, grass-roots opposition to Bush's war plans. Of 414 stories on the Iraqi problem that aired on NBC, ABC, and CBS from September 14, 2002, to February 7, 2003, Tyndall says only 34 stories originated from outside the White House, Pentagon or State Department.

British Broadcasting Corporation (BBC) Director-General Greg Dyke, for example, says many U.S. television networks abandoned neutrality during the war—with one even calling U.S. soldiers "heroes" and "liberators"—and thus risked losing all credibility. "Personally," he said, "I was shocked while in the United States by how unquestioning the broadcast news media were during this war. If Iraq proved anything, it was that the BBC cannot afford to mix patriotism and journalism. This is happening in the United States and, if it continues, will undermine the credibility of the U.S. electronic news media. For the health of our democracy, it's vital we don't follow the path of many American networks."

The liberal media watchdog group Fairness and Accuracy in Reporting (FAIR) reported some of the hard numbers of the media's coverage of the Iraq war. In a study performed in the first three weeks of the war (March 20 to April 9, 2003), FAIR researchers Steve Rendell and Tara Broughel reported that "official voices"—past and present leaders in the administration and military—dominated the TV news, having the effect of "squelching dissent" and squeezing out other views, including perspectives from abroad. U.S. TV watchers, the study says, "were more than six times as likely to see a pro-war source as one who was antiwar; on shows with U.S. guests alone, the ratio increases to 25 to 1." The researchers show that military commentators received twice as much attention as civilians did. Overall, they say, only 3% of U.S. sources "represented or expressed opposition to the war."

"With more than 1 in 4 U.S. citizens opposing the war," the report says, "and much higher rates of opposition in most countries where opinion was polled, none of the networks offered anything resembling proportionate coverage of antiwar voices. The antiwar percentages ranged from 4% at NBC, 3% percent at CNN, ABC, PBS, and Fox, and less than 1%—1 out of 205 U.S. sources—at CBS." Moreover, opinions against the war were almost always expressed in one-sentence sound bites, very often from someone simply labeled "protester" or "antiwar activist."

No, news broadcasters are just like the rest of us. They are ambitious and they want to succeed. They want airtime. And that means pleasing their bosses. The smart broadcasters saw that the wind was blowing from a new corporate-friendly direction, and they have blown with the wind. Again, during the Iraq War, it didn't take a genius to realize that the only welcome (and paid) guests on the news programs were primarily ex-generals from the military. The head of news programming for CNN was asked during a National Public Radio (NPR) interview if he would ever consider paying an antiwar activist to appear on his network as he had done with numerous retired military types, and he said that during wartime, he thought that would be un-American. You have to be concerned when it is considered "un-American" to speak out against war.

With regard to the content of the news, the new conservative corporate bias shows up not only in what is reported but also in what goes unreported. When was the last time you saw NBC run a news story critical of its parent, GE? Or has ABC ever done an expose on its corporate parent, Disney? A game theorist might argue that it is also unlikely that ABC would ever find fault with GE because GE might retaliate and find something critical of Disney to discuss on its NBC network. In fact, why would a corporate-owned news show be critical of any corporation? Aren't they all members of the same corporate family? Don't they all want the same things: low wages, open borders, free trade, less regulation, and less taxation? When was the last time *60 Minutes* aired a real hard-hitting expose of a Fortune 500 company?

And how much coverage have you seen critical of defense spending or the weapons systems that are funded by it? Did you ever see a program that analyzed the suggested elimination of the inheritance tax and who might benefit? The standard line that small farmers and small business owners were the prime beneficiaries turned out to be blatantly false. It was the super-wealthy who were the recipients of one of the biggest tax giveaways in America's history.

Why were these stories not covered? Because there was not enough airtime given all the prime-time news specials that focused on welfare cheats, deadbeat dads, Medicare rip-offs, illegal immigrants, school lunch price increases, and health care's rising costs. It seems the American government does not have the time or inclination to focus on these issues important to the common folk in

America, but the networks have plenty of time to dedicate to using America's poorest citizens as scapegoats for why the government can't balance a federal budget. The entire sum of money spent on welfare for the families with dependent children program was $64 billion a year at its peak. This is about what the defense department spends every couple of months!

It is sometimes argued that corporate and governmental affairs are not covered in depth because they just don't make good television viewing. Agreed, they do not have as much sex and violence as standard television fare, but it used to be that networks felt they had a public responsibility to air such news. In fact, it is a requirement of their maintaining their FCC licenses that they serve the public interest (U.S. Chamber of Commerce— National Telecommunications and Information Administration). They cannot give the same excuse, however, to explain their lack of coverage of antiwar and antiglobalization street protests around the country and the world. There has been no better television in recent years than the numerous antiwar and antiglobalization protests. They had it all. Unruly youth, energy, violence, blood, anarchists, police confrontations, fires, broken windows … everything, that is, but television coverage.

A good test of the reasonableness of your country's policies is to see how they are being viewed by other countries. Did you see anything other than snippets and sound bites of the antiwar protests occurring in most every major capital around the world? The largest single-day peaceful protest demonstration in human history occurred prior to the outbreak of hostilities in Iraq, and the networks couldn't make room for the story. As nearly 300,000 American, British, and Australian troops marched their way into Iraq, a much larger contingent of antiwar protestors took to the streets in every corner of the world. Peace marches were held in Canada, Australia, India, Thailand, Japan, and Pakistan. In the U.S., tens of thousands marched through many of the largest cities. An estimated 110,000 Italians, mostly students, flooded the streets of Rome as the war began. More than 100,000 demonstrated in Athens, Greece (*Macleans,* 3/31/03). How much coverage did it receive on the news. A common trick is for a cable news channel to air the footage once, so they can say they aired it, and then air competing footage supportive of the war hundreds of times in a weekend.

The mere fact that corporations are in the business of making money adds a distinct bias to news reporting. First of all, since the corporations' takeover, each of the news departments is now considered a profit center, whereas before it was understood each was providing a public service and typically ran at a loss. The immediate impact of this change in philosophy was that most of the networks had dramatic reductions in staffing. This meant fewer independent reporters covering and interpreting an event and more sharing of news feeds between the networks. In his few and far between press conferences, President Bush regularly calls on the same journalists who he knows ask safe questions, thus excluding questions from more controversial commentators.

More important, corporate ownership and a focus on profits changed the overall philosophy of the news departments. They now had to worry about ratings and viewership. It was if the movie *Network* had suddenly come to life in all its splendor. News departments were being taken over by programming people, news was being treated like entertainment, and everything was as predicted in the movie except the fortuneteller doing the nightly weather report utilizing her crystal ball. In a development even the movie couldn't have anticipated, in the Iraq war, embedded journalists' constant reporting turned the war into the ultimate in reality programming. Unlike Vietnam reporting, which shocked Americans with the horrors of war by bringing the casualties into their living rooms, dispatches from Iraq were polite enough to censure any real signs of death and suffering but filled Americans' televisions with heart-warming stories of patriotism and military commitment. In-depth reporting was replaced by flashy, short sound bites. Stories were condensed to less than 30 seconds, the networks' calculation of their audience's average attention span. Journalists were replaced with newsreaders. News editors were replaced by handsome anchors. And pictures of the horror of war were replaced with a wall of family photos of our beloved armed forces, each associated with a heartwarming story to make us feel warm and fuzzy as we killed thousands of Iraqis.

A dangerous precedent was established. A news show concerned with profits and ratings also had to be concerned with the quality of its interviews. The networks had to maintain access to the best talking heads, the biggest corporate executives, and the highest office holders in the government. The news departments quickly learned that the way to maintain "access", their life-blood, was to be nice to their interview guests. No hard-hitting questions, no accusations, no surprises—in effect, no journalism. The nicer the interviewer, the higher the probability that he or she would continue to have access in the future and the greater the viewership and therefore the profitability. In this environment, no one would want to acquire a reputation as a tough interviewer. Even Sam Donaldson tried to soften up in his post-Nixon days, but his forced smile is so artificial that one can see it hasn't been easy. The venerable Mike Wallace was stretched to the limit; if the movie *The Insider* is at all accurate, he was shown folding to tobacco company pressure by pulling a *60 Minutes* report critical of the industry.

Programming and even news content are steered by the demographics of the audience media executives want to attract. And what group has the best demographic profile for advertisers? The rich! So news became news that rich people wanted to see, and sometimes a bias slipped in to make that news more palatable to the rich. Cable news channels became constant ticker tapes, concerned solely with how the Dow Jones was doing that hour. It never occurred to anyone that the Dow Jones measured only investors' wealth and not the workers' well-being. Entire programs and even some entire cable channels became dedicated to reviewing stock market data and the companies that composed it. Economic reporting dwarfed all other types of reporting as if to say that if it didn't affect the Dow, it must not be much of a problem. When was the last time you saw a report on the national news about the inner cities, the rural poor, the concerns of our institutionalized elderly, complaints from prisons' inmates, or the state of the poor in the developing world? It just doesn't affect the average stock portfolio. Americans are much more compassionate, generous, and sympathetic than their television shows exhibit. But their target audience, the wealthiest Americans, may not be.

Still other profit motivations make for bad news reporting. The corporations that own the media are always concerned about limiting liability from defamation and slander lawsuits, so the logical precaution is never to defame anyone. This ensures that nothing controversial will ever be asked or aired.

Obviously, a general pro-consumption and pro-growth message is important not only for pleasing corporate owners of the media in general but for selling ad time specifically. A different view is that the general trash the networks put out as entertainment, including reality programming, sitcoms, and game shows, acts as the modern opiate of the masses. If the American public watches, it is hard to blame the networks. But networks have not acted as the guiding light to an enlightened new offering of culture and the arts on television.

The conservatives' dominance of radio is also interesting. Rush Limbaugh has done enormous damage to the spirit of free discourse with his polarizing and damning generalizations of the left and liberal politics. It is not just his philosophy that is extreme. He has made it acceptable to lie in defending one's positions. What can you say about talk show radio programming that features convicted felons Oliver North and G. Gordon Liddy as hosts of their own daily programs? And why do these talk show hosts attack the media as liberal? It allows them and their listeners o ignore any news that controverts their right-wing theories by denigrating the quality of the news source.

We might get more intelligent and unbiased programming by dedicating more resources to television's Public Broadcasting System (PBS) and radio's NPR, but these media outlets are not without fault. Because they feel they have to combat the conservative and corporate bias of the general for-profit media, they sometimes bend over backward and often suffer from extreme liberal bias. During the Iraq war, NPR scoured the country looking for guests who would be critical of the war effort. If the corporate bias of the mainstream media were straightened out, perhaps this reactive bias of the public media might correct itself.

Although there is no formal advertising on PBS, corporations may sponsor an entire program and receive on-air acknowledgement. PBS is probably less likely to air an expose of the huge subsidies going to agribusiness and ethanol production given that Archers Daniels Midland is one of its biggest sponsors. This problem too might go away if proper levels of public funding for public television and radio could be attained. Is it ironic that U.S. taxpayers pay to beam news free into repressive regimes but do not adequately fund their own news efforts at home? Of course, the inadequate funding did not occur by mistake; it was a central element of the Republican congress's Contract with America in 1994. Originally, some die-hards wanted to cut funding altogether, but eventually they settled on leaving public broadcasting barely breathing on life support. The message got through. If public TV and radio maintained their liberal bias, further cuts were possible.

While public television and radio is in much better shape in Europe, there too it is coming under attack. Private media is launching an ambitious attempt to restrict public media's operations and to seek a cutback on its government funding. While limiting the for-profit activities of these public broadcasters may be appropriate, most likely conservative business owners will attempt to curtail their news operations. Europe only has to look to America to see how dangerous it is to silence the voice of public broadcasting.

So what damage has been done to America's democracy by the corporate takeover and consolidation of its media? An incalculable amount. How many wonderful books have never seen the light of day because they were not written by big-name establishment types or media personalities? What news is being censured by corporate entertainment executives? Who at these corporations is giving the green light to new movie scripts, and what would they think of a documentary critical of American corporations? (Why did the movie *The Insider* open to such rave reviews, generate big initial box office numbers and then not spend the necessary advertising dollars to successfully roll out the picture to an even bigger audience?).

When corporations interfered with our news media, they damaged the fundamental fabric of America's democracy and its constitutional guarantees of individual freedom. The impact is already being felt, but its long-term effects can only be guessed. The news media are our eyes and ears to government, corporations, and the world. If the images they provide are distorted, the damage is difficult to see and even more difficult to correct. While it is disturbing to see the problems inherent in our government, our businesses and our democracy, it is even more disturbing to realize that our media has been co-opted. It is hard to imagine how this message will ever reach a popular audience if our media opposes it.

Summary and Conclusion

The revolution will not go better with Coke.
The revolution will not be televised.

GIL SCOTT-HERON

12

THE CITIZENS' AGENDA AND CONCLUSION

If corporate and other elites have undue influence on the government's policies, there should be two recognizable symptoms. First, as discussed previously, many of the items on the special interests' wish lists should be coming true. Low corporate taxes, elimination of inheritance taxes, reduction in personal income taxes on the wealthy, weakened product liability protections for consumers, lower union participation, and industrial globalization without protection for workers' rights and the environment all seem to point to the fact that the lobbyists' wishes are indeed being fulfilled.

But second, and as important, if corporate and other elites have too much say in the government, that must mean that average citizens have too little say. One would expect to find issues of importance to average Americans being ignored by their government. Government representatives know what all Americans know: The average American never contributes one dollar to a political campaign and rarely, if ever, goes to Washington to lobby his or her elected representatives. Consider this then a people's agenda—the problems the people's representatives in Washington and the state capital might tackle if the special interests ever got out of Washington and elected officials started working for the people for a change. They may not seem as major as famines and war, but to every citizen who has to work hard to earn a living in America, they can be enormously annoying and deserve some attention from government to see if a solution can be found.

As for America's problems at home, they will begin to take care of themselves as the people's issues are discussed in government without the corrupting bias of special interests. Without the AARP's involvement, Social Security problems might be addressed immediately. Conversion of the Social Security system to make it needs based would immediately make it solvent again, would provide benefits to those who need them most, and would lower the payroll tax burden on the working middle class and poor. The teachers' union and school administrators stand in the way of schools' improving immediately because of their entrenched positions on staffing and performance-based pay. Innovative programs like vouchers usable only in public schools might be tested. And without corporate America's dominance of the political process, real progress could be made on pollution, global warming, living wage programs, alternative energy plans, better and more affordable health care, reasonably priced pharmaceutical drugs, and new antitrust laws to prevent price gouging.

If Roll and Talbott (2003) are right about democracy's importance in creating a healthy broad-based economy, economic miracles should start happening as soon as political power is returned to the people. Once elites and corporations are removed from politics, our government will be back in the business of helping average Americans economically. Tax burdens could be lifted from the working poor and middle class as a greater share of the charge is shifted to the wealthiest citizens. Inheritance taxes on the wealthy could be reestablished so that all children have the same opportunity for success. With the tax system corrected, government deficits would disappear and citizens could enact limits on government spending and total borrowing. Bottom line, the economy would explode. Steady 6% to 7% growth each year in the economy will be easy to achieve once people are excited about investing and working again, our government is straightened out and our economy encourages participation by all.

But the miracles would not cease there. Smaller issues that never make it onto the radar screen of our representatives would finally be addressed by our government. Spam emails would disappear from personal computers, computer viruses would be better controlled and there would be protections implemented to prevent the elderly from having to suffer from abusive marketing pitches for products they don't want.

Banks form an incredibly powerful lobbying force in Washington. Without their undue influence, there would be a major investigation of the countless fees that banks force their customers to pay. The government also needs to do a better job regulating the credit reporting industry. The insurance industry regulations would be tightened and brokerage houses would be restrained from lying to their customers.

Society will be less inundated with advertising for alcohol, tobacco, and gambling once these industries lose their political influence. While outright prohibition probably makes little sense, there is no reason these industries have to be continually advertising and pushing their products on us and our children.

Americans have lived so long in a topsy-turvy world where corporations had so much clout in Washington that it sounds funny to even discuss what a political world would look like if America had a government that was responsive solely to the people. Having a government that is responsive to the needs of all its people need not be bad for the economy. Such a government, unlike a corporate-dominated system, would value justice and fairness and show genuine compassion for its citizens. And for those few who continue to break the laws, this responsive government would find a way to deal with them in a strong but compassionate manner that we hope would have better results than the present prison system.

You can easily see how the symptoms of a rather sick society that were described in the first chapter might begin to improve quickly if these changes were enacted. People might regain some faith in their government and their business leaders if they felt the game was not rigged for those at the top. As they reasserted their political power, they might gain a new appreciation of their communities and their neighbors. The veil of loneliness, insularity, and negativism may lift from the people and be replaced with the can-do American ethic that once made this country great and will do so again!

To summarize the major findings of this text, first, democratic institutions are an important ingredient to a well-functioning society. The popular vote, civil liberties, and a free press backed by a strong constitution and a bill of rights ensuring individual liberty are important for the preservation of the freedoms they provide individuals in a society. They act to prevent overly ambitious governments from constraining individual liberties and as a self-policing mechanism to ensure that government is effective and efficient in performing all its duties.

But just as important, democratic institutions are enormously beneficial to the adoption and maintenance of a free market economy. Almost all the wealthiest countries of the world are free market democracies while many of those countries that lag in economic performance are autocratic in nature or have done a poor job adjusting to democracy.

Democratic institutions fill this need in monitoring the government, which, when it is working properly, polices the economy and its market participants. The free press keeps the people current with relevant information about how the government is doing; the people exercise their right to organize and assemble peacefully when they want to provide timely vocal feedback to the government. Citizens hold the ultimate trump card, the vote, to turn out government officials who either don't listen or are ineffective in their response. Good government results in a growing economy.

Poorly run governments can do many things to damage an economy including; running huge deficits, creating unmanageable inflation, ignoring property rights, causing unnecessary regulation to harm business formation, closing borders to trade and new ideas, mismanaging their currencies, and so on. If citizens vote their pocketbook, they will be interested in electing representatives who put policies in place that will generate economic growth. Only through economic growth can the poor escape poverty and the country have the necessary resources to educate its children, care for the disadvantaged and care for its sick and elderly. Once the proper policies are established, democratic institutions act as watchdogs to ensure that the policies are followed in the future.

Governments, if properly structured, perform a unique function for their citizens. There is no reason for government to conduct business that could more efficiently be conducted by the private sector. The businesses to which government should restrict itself are these:

- Formation of fundamental institutions such as property rights and the rule of law

- The setting of standards of fairness, justice, and generosity

- The allocation of non-economic goods and services, or those goods and services that citizens feel the free market does a poor job of allocating

It makes little sense to conduct such business in the unregulated private market, but the government should use as many free-market tools as possible to ensure that it performs the service in a cost-efficient manner. It is ironic that as countries develop greater and greater inequality of income, more and more goods and services lend themselves to government allocation because people feel uncomfortable letting the richest citizens grab a bigger share of these important goods based solely on their wealth. Unfortunately, this leads to larger inefficiencies in the distribution of goods and services because governments are rarely as efficient as private industry.

Before Americans set out to change the world, they might want to do a little introspection to see if their own democracy is as healthy and functioning as our founders intended. The United States, long held in admiration as one of the most venerable of the world's democracies, is beginning to show some cracks. America's leaders are making decisions for its people with little open debate and democratic feedback from the citizenry. The country has decided to pull out of the Kyoto Accords on global warming, to abstain from an international effort to try war criminals, and to invade a previously defeated developing country, all with very little discussion or feedback from its citizens and the other democracies of the world.

What has gone wrong with democracy in America? Most of the problem can be traced back to the unresponsiveness of the government to its people. Unfortunately, special interests have taken over the American government. This is a clear violation of the principle of one person/one vote that states that each citizen ought to have equal access and say in the running of our government. Allowing special interests, special access, and undue influence violates this first rule of fairness. But there are more important consequences as well.

Each special interest has its own self-interest. The business of government is concerned with the public interest, but rather than allowing that work to be done, the special interest often distorts the process to accomplish its narrow self-interest. Beyond just a simple violation of fairness, this damages the entire governmental process and leads to a breakdown of democratic governance. The reason is simple. Citizens watching this process realize it is not just and they lose confidence in their government. As they pull away, they take with them the citizen involvement that is essential for a well-functioning democracy and economy.

In addition, solving complex collective action problems that government is supposed to be good at becomes impossible when decision makers are asked to report to individuals and corporations that do not have the general public's interests at heart. What sense does it make to ask a corporation how much tax it would like to pay or how much regulation it wants? Corporations perceive poorly how to satisfy the general public good, nor should they; they should act solely in their narrow economic self-interest. But it is for exactly this reason that they should be prohibited from participating in the political process. Corporate lobbying and corporate campaign contributions should be eliminated.

Free markets and corporations do a wonderful job in the economic marketplace of creating value, organizing people to complete complex endeavors, and allocating resources. It is just that they are very poorly suited, regardless of their economic power to effect change in the political world. Corporate interests do not align well with those of individuals. While both would like to see increasing profits and a rising stock market, people would most likely take exception to a plan that lowers wages, reduces consumer product quality or product safety, limits corporate responsibility and liability, restricts employee health care and pension benefits, or ships jobs overseas. Not all people are wealthy investors, and given how far-flung American corporate operations are now around the world, what is good for GM these days is not necessarily good for Americans.

So what do corporations get in return for their political contributions and lobbying efforts? To start with, many receive tax breaks equal to hundreds of times the amount of their dollar contributions. But this is only the tip of the iceberg. The laundry list of corporate benefits due to their unjust influence in Washington is extensive and includes barriers to union organizing, price support help, tariff protection, preservation of monopoly status, import protection, liberal export policies, liability protection and restrictions on mandatory employee benefits including health care provisions.

We said that eliminating onerous or unnecessary regulation is good for a growing economy, but when big corporations are making the rules, this is not what occurs. The burdensome regulation stays in place to act as a disincentive to any entrepreneur that might want to challenge the market leadership position of the big corporation. Instead, the regulations that are eliminated are the valuable rules that keep the market fair and honest.

The wealthy who try to influence the government have a similar agenda. Their primary motivation is to reduce their taxes, even if it means damaging the economy. You will see them lobbying for reduced income taxes, reduced capital gains taxes, and an elimination of the inheritance tax, but they show much less concern for taxes that are a burden on the poor and middle class such as state and local sales taxes and Social Security payroll taxes.

Because wealthy people are primarily investors or business owners, most of their income comes from investments rather than wages, and their interests on business issues align quite nicely with corporate interests. They are all for keeping wages and benefits down, removing restrictions on corporate operations, and eliminating any regulations that seek to protect consumers, workers, or the environment and might raise the cost of doing business.

There are many other special interests trying to influence the government with money and lobbying efforts. They pale in comparison to the efforts of the biggest corporations and wealthiest citizens, but they can still be enormously damaging because they concentrate their energies on issues directly affecting them. Americans seem to turn to people and organizations that are closest and most familiar with a problem to help solve it, forgetting that these same organizations have a self-serving bias that prevents a solution optimal to the general public. Whether talking about the AARP's addressing the Social Security issue, teachers and school administrators' trying to improve the schools, or lawyers' reflecting on improvements in tort reform, each group has its own agenda, which is nothing like the public's agenda. They therefore act as impediments to finding a solution or their lobbying efforts result in solutions that are less than ideal from the general public's perspective.

Another strong indicator that something is terribly wrong with America comes in the form of feedback from foreign nations. The Arabs hate us because of our unconditional support for Israel. Our European allies think less of us because America seems to be going off on its own more without consulting them. Countries in the developing world see that America forces their borders open to trade but keeps American industries protected from the developing world's exports. Americans have pushed an agenda of unregulated free markets on the world through the WTO and the IMF with no consideration of its effect on workers, wages, the environment, or the health and welfare of the world's people.

We have identified some fairly straightforward actions that a developing country ought to take if it wants to prosper economically:

- Enact a democratic constitutional form of government
- Promote the rule of law and protection of property rights
- Minimize unnecessary government regulation
- Stop printing money and running big deficits
- Open borders to new ideas and trade
- Institute democratic reforms including the popular vote, freedom of speech and guaranteed civil liberties

There is a dilemma for people of well-intentioned advanced countries who wish to see the suffering and oppression end in autocratic regimes. Many have a natural abhorrence to violence and war, and it seems reasonable that pressure on dictatorships should come from a democratically elected international body, composed solely of the democratic countries of the world. But short of invasion or threat of assassination, it is hard to see why a ruthless dictator would abdicate. Any economic sanctions would probably just hurt the citizens of the country rather than the dictator.

Finally, you ask why there hasn't been more written about this crippling of America's government by special interests or why we haven't heard more about it on the news. Corporations have infiltrated not only the government but universities and news media outlets as well. Once the finest minds in business get in bed with the finest minds in government, academia, and the media, there are few places to turn to find out what is really happening.

And what of the future? The focus in this book is primarily on isolating the problem infecting our government, our economy, and our society and on developing a better understanding of its causes. This is an important first step toward change because people have to see how unfair and unjust the world is today and to understand who the offenders are before we can expect them to become outraged. And public outrage is the only vehicle that will lead to success in stopping these anti-democratic forces in America and around the world.

Can we be optimistic that change for the better will come? This is a difficult question. The biggest special interests in America are some of the most powerful business, economic, and political interests in the world. If the media has sold out to big business, the traditional communications channels needed to organize any people's revolt will have been taken away. How can people feel revulsion toward something unjust if they don't even hear about it?

Of course there is always the Internet. Although the Internet failed to create permanent dot-com billionaires in the business sector, it may still be an extremely powerful force in the political world. Web sites such as www.moveon.org have been shown to be very effective tools for political organizing with letter-writing campaigns to Congress and get-out-the-vote initiatives. In the long run, history seems to demonstrate that good always triumphs over evil. People will eventually find a way, even if it means starting new neighborhood newspapers and radio stations, forming new political parties, or eventually refusing to participate in a corrupted system. Mohandas Gandhi said, "Almost anything you do will be insignificant, but it is very important that you do it." Remember, if you are feeling powerless, that these big corporations depend on us to buy their products. The word "boycott" will put the fear of God into all of them.

We have these hopes:

- To introduce publicly financed campaigns

- To take corporations out of the political influence business

- To limit the groups that can lobby the government

- To depend to a much greater extent on direct referenda on issues affecting all Americans

- To severely punish the elected officials who corruptly act in any way other than on behalf of the public interest

We also hope that those in academia will voluntarily come to their senses and realize their critical independence is threatened. If they do, we will see to it that the best-funded, highest-quality, publicly-owned news media are available on television and radio in every great city of our country by actively supporting publicly-owned television and radio. Finally, we will support democracy around the world as the last best hope of humankind to end the suffering of billions of poverty-stricken people and allow them the freedom and dignity they are justly due.

We have tried to describe the powerful impact such changes will have on politics, our government, our society, our economy, and our people. It will be so pervasive and so powerful and it will unleash such good that it is almost impossible to adequately describe. People will believe in the system once again. People will work hard, children will become excited about learning, and families will invest in their futures again because they know the rules of the game are fair and just. And the American people, for the first time in a very long time, will trust one another again and build meaningful, close, and productive human relationships. While market competition leads to productive and efficient work, it is only through cooperation that humanity unleashes its true greatness and finds the fullness in life available in a community of friends and neighbors. Now that is the America, and that is the world that we envision!

Appendix

POLITICAL FREEDOM, ECONOMIC LIBERTY, AND PROSPERITY

Richard Roll and John R. Talbott

Why do some countries display economic vitality and growth, while others stagnate at low levels of output? Why are only a few of the so-called developing countries actually developing? There is little variation in human DNA across the world and thus little variation in basic human nature. This suggests that the enormous economic

Richard Roll holds the Japan Alumni Chair in International Finance at the Anderson Graduate School of Management at UCLA. He is past president of the American Finance Association and is a fellow of the Econometric Society. John Talbott, the author of this book, is a former investment banker for Goldman, Sachs & Co. and visiting scholar at the Anderson School at UCLA. A longer version of this research paper, including detailed descriptions and explanations of all empirical findings, is available at www.anderson.ucla.edu/acad_unit/finance/wp/2001/19-01.pdf.

Reprinted from *Journal of Democracy* 14, 3, July 2003, 75–89.

differences are caused, at least to some extent, by politically determined local conditions, and raises the highly practical question of what, if anything, governments can do to speed development.

The vast amount of academic research on this topic shows that it fascinates scholars. More importantly, it is critical for our planet. Approximately 80 percent of all humans live in poverty. The poorest one billion among them must get by on less than $2 a day.

Many studies have attempted to explain the variations in economic growth from country to country and over time, but identifying meaningful and significant correlations between growth rates and potential explanatory variables is hard, for several reasons.[1] Gross National Income per capita (GNIpc) is much less volatile than growth as a measure of economic well being, but still has the requisite wide variance across countries needed to make our findings potentially significant.

When asking how governments can foster development, it makes no sense to consider exogenous physical variables such as latitude; to call for reformation of religious beliefs, ethnicity, and culture; or to wring one's hands about wars, colonial periods, and other events in the past. Similarly, no government bent on improvement needs to be told to "acquire more capital and better technology": These are well-known correlates of wealth (indeed they may be as much its tokens as its causes), and pointing to their significance provides no guide to action. Instead, one *must* focus on the macroeconomic, structural, political, and institutional conditions that any government, working within the constraints of immutable circumstance, can act upon in order to maximize incomes for its people. The one thing most needful is to uncover the deep determinants of development that actually drive more proximate factors.

To obtain proxies for these deep determinants, we used data from well-known published sources[2] in order to come up with a possible list of 14 deep determinants of GNIpc. (As noted above in our biographical note, a full version of this essay with all the statistical tables summarizing our empirical findings is posted at *www.anderson.ucla.edu/acad_unit/finance/wp/2001/19-01.pdf.* The present essay will occasionally refer by number to tables that can be viewed at this location.)

As a group, our empirical proxies explain between 81 and 85 percent of the cross-country variation in GNIpc over five sample years (1995–99). Nine of the original 14 explanatory variables are statistically significant in every year.[3] In each case, a plus (+) or minus (–) sign indicates whether the variable correlates positively or negatively with higher GNIpc.

Property Rights (+), Informal Market Activity (–), and Regulation (-) have the highest levels of statistical significance. This points to the importance of knowing the rules of the game and being confident that the rules will be enforced. Political Rights (+), Civil Liberties (+), and Freedom of the Press (+) are also highly significant, supporting Milton Friedman's original claim that economic development seems to go hand-in-hand with political freedom.[4] Three other variables are also significant: Monetary Policy or Inflation (–), Trade Barriers (–), and Government Expenditures (+) as a percentage of GDP.

Surprisingly, though Trade Barriers represent a significant drag on GNIpc, actual trade levels (exports as a percentage of GDP) are insignificant. This suggests that trade barriers proxy for factors unrelated to trade itself. Corruption comes to mind because trade barriers, by distorting import and export prices, tend to encourage smuggling and the bribery of customs officials that goes with it.

It appears that the critical ingredient of a successful development policy is a fair and just system that invites profitable economic exchange among participants, with no risk of expropriation or repudiation. Effective government is essential—the significant explanatory variables reflect collective actions that no individual entrepreneur can provide alone. Once a developing country's government establishes fair rules of the game and ensures their enforcement, that government is well advised to interfere minimally with privately generated growth.

Table A.1 The most significant variables explaining country incomes (t-statistics)

	1999	1998	1997	1996	1995
Property Rights	12.61	12.34	9.75	10.00	9.46
Regulation	−5.08	−6.77	−3.77	−6.03	−4.89
Informal Market Activity	−11.08	−7.34	−7.90	−9.42	−9.51
Political Rights	3.84	2.05	2.69	3.47	3.99
Civil Liberties	5.28	2.96	3.77	4.65	5.29
Freedom of the Press	7.16	4.69	4.47	5.94	5.84
Trade Barriers	−6.26	−6.46	−8.73	−4.79	−7.24
Government Expenditures	5.49	5.32	5.36	2.98	1.13
Monetary Policy	−7.89	−8.00	−7.84	−8.49	−7.04
Adjusted R-square	**84.6%**	**81.9%**	**81.8%**	**82.9%**	**81.9%**
Number of Countries	**157**	**156**	**148**	**142**	**134**

Using readily available data from recognized sources,[5] we did a regression analysis that produced the following list of the most significant variables and the direction of their estimated impact on GNIpc (see Table A.1).

These variables are characterized both by high levels of statistical significance and by directional impacts which comport well with the idea that economic and political freedoms provide a friendly environment for healthy and growing economies. Milton Friedman might have predicted that trade barriers, inflation, and excessive regulation harm development, but he also would have encouraged the expansion of property rights, political rights, civil liberties and freedom of the press. The negative coefficient attached to informal economic activity probably reflects citizens' attempts to avoid burdensome regulation or overcome the drawbacks occasioned by poorly enforced property rights.

The only mild surprise on the list of significant variables is government expenditures, which has a positive coefficient. Policy makers in less-developed lands should probably not conclude from this that they can spend their way to prosperity. Perhaps a more sensible interpretation is that a developing country's ability to collect taxes and provide government services indicates a well-organized state, while developed countries typically spend more on defense and transfer payments.

Weaving a tale around the bare statistics of a regression should be an exercise in caution. Authors have biases and data can be flawed. Nonetheless, we feel obliged to offer an interpretation, first by discussing each highly significant explanatory variable, and then offering some general conclusions regarding the overall results.

Property Rights, Regulation, and the Informal Economy

The relations between per capita income and, respectively, Property Rights, Informal Market Activity, and Regulation are very strong across the cross-section of countries. This suggests that given strong property rights and a well-functioning judicial system, enterprising entrepreneurs could probably find adequate labor and capital. A lack of capital would represent an unusual profit opportunity for an aggressive and clever entrepreneur. With adequate property rights, developing countries might not require much external assistance, with all of its drawbacks.[6] Their economies could percolate up from the inside. If the rulebook of capitalism is stable, fair, and enforced, perhaps energetic self-interest will find the path of accelerated development.

The weak state of property rights in many less-developed countries not only discourages investment, diverts energy into smuggling, and renders external assistance problematic, but also puts a damper on the small businesses whose enterprises might otherwise be crucial engines of growth. In the world's largest economy—that of the United States—more than two-thirds of the new jobs created each year come in industries where small businesses (defined as having fewer than 50 employees) predominate. When entrepreneurs can feel confident that the fruits of their efforts will be safeguarded by a strong system of property rights, the appetite for work and risk-taking will be whetted. Where property rights are weak, the reverse applies. As the Peruvian economist Hernando de Soto explains:[7]

"The poor inhabitants of these (developing) nations—five-sixths of humanity—do have things, but they lack the process to represent their property and create capital. They have houses but not titles; crops but not deeds; businesses but not statutes of incorporation. It is the unavailability of these essential representations that explains why people who have adopted every other western invention, from the paper clip to the nuclear reactor, have not been able to produce sufficient capital to make domestic capitalism work."

De Soto goes on to say that in an informal economy (i.e., one with an inadequate or dysfunctional legal structure, even for licit economic activities) people commonly lack titles to their homes or businesses, cannot secure loans, cannot find insurance, cannot hook up utilities, and have no incentive to improve their property because they are unlikely to be able to realize much of a return from it.

It is interesting to note that in addition to Property Rights and Informal Activity, one of the statistically relevant variables in our analysis is Regulation. De Soto explains that excessive regulation forces individuals to conduct business informally.[8] De Soto recounts how, in Lima, Peru, it took 728 bureaucratic steps to acquire legal title to a home, while registering a new business took 280 days (in the United States, it typically takes an afternoon). Such excessive regulation usually has little or nothing to do with guarding the public interest, and is actually a form of rent-seeking in which existing (often upper- and middle-class) business owners collude with government employees to suppress competition from poorer, start-up entrepreneurs.

How large is this informal sector? In 2000, De Soto estimated it at US$9.3 trillion worldwide.[9] This is a staggeringly large number, and outside the national accounting system of the countries (so it would not appear in official GNIpc). But the very conditions that create the informal sector—unfair and excessive regulations and feeble rights to one's own property—also might tend it to stagnate. Growth cannot come without capital, and capital will not come without formal ownership.

The Importance of Democratic Institutions

Perhaps not surprisingly, Political Rights, Civil Liberties, and Press Freedom are highly correlated with each other, for each is a hallmark of an open, democratic society. They are not, however, all measuring the exact same thing for in fact, each has an independent, strong, and positive influence on country income. Our empirical results confirm the strong relationship that Friedman and others posit between political freedom and economic development, though we cannot be sure from our regression analysis which is the cause and which the effect. Many believe that higher incomes make it possible for people to become better educated and more involved in their government, which would mean that higher incomes cause democracy.[10]

Could it be, however, that the reverse is true, that democracy causes higher incomes? Democratic institutions and institutionalized liberal practices such as freedoms of speech and the press allow citizens to provide feedback to government leaders about the effectiveness of policies and their impact on general welfare.[11] In an autocratic world with no independent news editorials, no street protests and no second party voting, it is exceedingly easy for the rulers to remain insulated from feedback about how government policies are affecting the economy. Such feedback is a significant driver of growth. Nobel Laureate Amartya Sen made one of the most startling economic discoveries of our generation when he found that no democracy in history had ever suffered a famine.[12] Famines, he points out, are economic events, not purely natural disasters like droughts. Even the worst can be avoided if leaders have sufficient, effective, and timely feedback from their citizens about real or perceived threats to their well-being. Only open, democratic systems can do this consistently. In fact, democracy thrives on such feedback, while undemocratic regimes most often actively stifle it.

In addition to crucial information flows, open democratic institutions also furnish means to reverse economically destructive policies that would be much harder to challenge in a dictatorship. One might think of democracy as a balance-of-power arrangement in which citizens empower government to enforce contracts and protect property rights—thus preventing the diversion of productive resources—but constrain government as well lest it become a prime diverter itself, expropriating property and repudiating contracts.[13]

In an autocratic world, those with political power command multiple channels for diverting economic resources in ways that enrich a relative few but impoverish the many. Monopolies, currency manipulations, caps on domestic agricultural prices, and overstaffed and overpaid government bureaucracies, as well as outright bribery, extortion, and corruption are all methods that autocrats use to tax average citizens and transfer wealth to friends. Many developing countries have potent constituencies of government employees, workers and executives in protected industries, and landed aristocrats who prop up the existing system to the detriment of democratic reform and economic development.

War can be a more immediate and disastrous economic result of maintaining too much power in too few hands. A dictator can start a war on the slightest pretext. The citizenry, though at risk, has no voice. This is not the case in a democracy. One of the most striking features of modern history is the near total lack of warfare between developed liberal democracies.[14]

A curious, and rather small subset of autocracies have a "benevolent dictator" who more or less has the general interest at heart. But the problems here are well-known: All dictators claim to be benevolent; there is no assurance that the benevolence will continue;[15] even a truly well-meaning dictator will tend to suffer from the crippling lack of feedback discussed above; and a well-intentioned but inept dictator, unlike a democratic leader who is doing poorly, cannot easily be turned out of power.

Other Significant Variables

Other significant variables in our model are Monetary Policy, Trade Barriers, and Government Expenditures. To quantify Monetary Policy, we used the weighted average of a country's inflation rate for the last ten years. High inflation often comes because of pressures to print currency in order to fund a large budget deficit, which in turn is often the result of a badly run central government. Thus high inflation rates may be a proxy for poor governance.

Trade Barriers also seem to drag down growth to a statistically significant degree. This is no surprise, as scholars have stressed the importance of openness to commerce in achieving the comparative advantages of trade, and exposing a country to new ideas and new technologies.[16] Trade barriers, it should also be noted, not only discourage development by themselves, but also typically betoken what are essentially corrupt practices that defy the ideal of a "level playing field" for everyone (as when those in power "pay off" their allies in certain economic sectors with high tariffs designed to keep out competition from abroad). Thus the Trade Barriers variable does double duty, reflecting both a direct brake on development and underlying problems of governance that have the same effect.[17]

Perhaps surprisingly, the linear coefficient for Government Expenditures is positive and significant. At first, this might appear to debunk the view that government spending and taxation are impediments to free markets and growth. In advanced societies with substantial entitlement programs and transfer payments, governments might be a brake on economic activity. But many developing countries have just the opposite problem. They do not collect taxes efficiently, and thus have difficulty paying for the kinds of basic public services and infrastructure that people in developed countries take for granted. In this sense, these developing-country governments are spending too little. The overall evidence suggests that government spending at low levels is proxying for efficient government organization (such as in tax collecting and providing basic services), but that there is a level above which public spending becomes a drag on the economy.

Political Freedom and Growth:
Cause or Effect?

Does democracy breed development, or vice-versa? Which way the causal arrow is taken to point is a question of more than purely scientific interest; there are critical policy implications at stake. Unfortunately, there is no sure way to distinguished cause from effect using cross-sectional data; that issue can only be resolved when a country actually changes one or more "explanatory" variables and observes the effect, if any.

In every case, we have chosen candidate variables that actually are amenable to policy control, so that a confirming experiment is possible. To date, however, no country has offered itself as the guinea pig. There remains an alternative: Examine what happened in the past to country incomes when countries independently made such changes.

Conditions that might plausibly be effects of higher incomes include those associated with economic and political freedoms—namely, the conditions characteristic of free markets and democracy. The basic question is whether political and market reforms bring about economic conditions that lead to more rapid economic development; or conversely, whether exogenous improvements in income precede and precipitate better education and more informed citizens yearning for democracy. In other words, do self-rule and liberty make people prosper, or do they get rich first and then want freedom?

To resolve this issue, we borrowed the events-study method, a technique that financial economists have been using for decades to isolate the impact of a particular event in the life of a business corporation. The first events study, in 1969, examined how stock

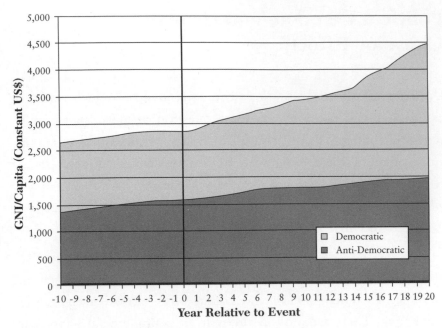

Figure A.1   Real per capita income around democratic and anti-democratic events (event is in year zero)

splits affect the market prices of stocks.[18] Since then, hundreds of such studies have since been published.

The event of interest here is a material change—up or down—in a country's level of political freedom. How does such a political shift affect economic growth? The two possible directions of change define distinct event categories. The first category includes events such as first-time-ever free elections, the toppling of a dictator, the addition to the ballot of a party or parties other than the ruling party, and the like. For want of a better term, we call these "democratic" events. The second category includes events such as a military coup, a dictatorial takeover, or the suspension of a constitution, all of which we term "anti-democratic." In identifying democratic and anti-democratic events we employed a rather mechanical approach by canvassing the 2001 *CIA World Factbook* to identify events in both categories.[19] To test the reasonableness of this approach, and to capture other events we had either missed or mis-characterized in our initial assessment, we asked Larry Diamond of the Hoover Institute to make additional revisions to our list. While his revisions resulted in the final reported results being slightly less supportive of our thesis, the statistical tests were still highly significant. Our list of democratic and anti-democratic events appears at the end of this article and is labeled Table A.2.

As Figure A.1 shows, democratic events have been followed by rather dramatic increases in GNIpc. The average sample country was experiencing little real growth in the five years prior to the event, approximately .67 percent per year, so there is little evidence of prior prosperity that might have triggered a move to democracy. After the event, these same countries began to grow rapidly. In the first five years, they accelerated to an annual rate of 2.2 percent. This was followed by an annual rate of 1.7 percent in the next five years and then to 2.7 percent in the subsequent decade. To conclude that the event itself was *not* causative, one would be forced to rely on a truly convoluted story; namely, that the mere *anticipation* of future prosperity impelled citizens to hector their government into reforming. Moreover, the quantitative impact is enormous. To put it in perspective, a 2.7 percent annual rate of real growth in GNIpc is enough to double per capita real income every 26 years. To the extent that such reforms become effective today, all the countries of the world could be out of poverty within the lifetimes of their youngest children.

Countries in the anti-democratic event sample had been experiencing fairly decent growth during the decade prior to the event, averaging 1.6 percent growth per annum. Afterward, growth declined by approximately half in the second five-year period after the event and continued at that depressed rate of approximately .85 percent per year for the second decade after the event.

Moreover, in no subperiod after the events did their growth rate approach the level enjoyed by countries that experienced a democratic event.

The pattern displayed in Figure A.1 constitutes compelling evidence that democracy-related changes by a country's government *cause* changes in per capita income.

For several reasons, the two event categories need not be mirror images. One reason is that countries in the anti-democratic sample had generally lower wealth prior to the event, possibly due to negative prior experiences such as colonization or civil war, which also might have precipitated the accession of dictators. In addition, democratic features such as a free press and civil liberties are not the only causative factors behind rapid development; property rights, trade barriers, monetary policy, and government expenditures have some explanatory power. Nor is an anti-democratic event inevitably followed by uniformly poor policy choices. A good example is Chile, whose democratically elected Marxist government was ousted by a military coup in 1973. Chile thereafter had a dictator, but a rare one who adopted relatively enlightened economic policies including a respect for property rights.

Across our entire sample, the average country experiencing a democratic event had approximately 80 percent higher income prior to the event than the average country experiencing an anti-democratic event, albeit both had average incomes that would be considered quite low by advanced country standards. It might be argued that a threshold level of income, and possibly education, must be attained before democratic events are likely. We admit that this is a compelling argument, but it does not negate our findings about causality. Whenever such events occur for any reason, more rapid economic development follows soon thereafter. True, democratic events might be easier to bring about in richer countries, but wealth is clearly not a theoretically necessary condition and many democratic events actually have occurred in poor countries.

Missing Determinants?

Another potentially serious problem of any cross-sectional analysis is the unintentional omission of important influences. Given the events study just described, one obvious candidate for an omitted variable is the elapsed time since a country has undergone a democratic event. Such events precipitate rapid growth, but it still takes time to achieve a high *level* of GNIpc. Inclusion of the elapsed time since a democratic event weakens, but does not eliminate, the statistical significance of the three other democracy-related variables: political rights, civil liberties, and press freedom. Given that all four variables measure democratic conditions, this is not too surprising, and it does not, of course, moderate the basic conclusion that democratic conditions cause high incomes. None of the other significant variables is affected; in particular, trade barriers, property rights, black market activities, regulation, monetary policy, and government spending are all virtually unaltered.

Although we cannot prove it unequivocally, we strongly suspect that another seemingly omitted variable involves measurement error in GNI itself. The GNIpc data were adjusted in the original sources in an effort to portray true standards of living across countries. This is, of course, an exceedingly difficult task. Fortunately, since pure measurement error is random noise, it is not likely to affect the coefficients or statistical significance of other explanatory variables. In partial confirmation, we show that proxies for measurement error do not materially influence the significance pattern of our original 14 determinants.

Conclusion

Data for 1995 through 1999 indicate that more than 80 percent of the cross-country variation in wealth (GNIpc) can be explained by nine separate influences. The most significant and consistent positive influences are strong property rights, political rights, civil liberties, press freedom, and government expenditures. The negative significant influences include excessive regulation, poor monetary policy, informal economic activity, and trade barriers.

When countries undertake a democratic change such as deposing a dictator, they enjoy a rather dramatic spurt in economic growth, which persists for at least two decades. In contrast, an anti-democratic event is followed by a reduction in growth. This verifies that democratic conditions really are *causes* of cross-country differences in wealth and not the endogenous effects of wealth. There are indeed crucial local conditions for economic development, conditions that can actually be established by a progressive government on behalf of its citizens.

Each statistically significant variable in our model contributes to the explanation of cross-country differences in per capita income. But is there anything that these seemingly disparate variables share in common? There does appear to be a common thread, or rather two of them. First, these variables represent institutions and policies that promulgate clearly understood and enforced laws and rules. The rules must be applied equitably and consistently. The underlying rulebook principles are fairness and justice. Economic participants cannot save in a world of hyperinflation caused by governments that debauch the currency rather than behave responsibly. They cannot compete with state-sponsored monopolies. They cannot trade efficiently with the existence of high tariffs and phony official exchange rates. They cannot easily overcome burdensome regulation and corruption. They cannot capitalize future profits in a world devoid of property rights. And the ideal prosperous state of personal and economic freedom cannot survive for long without the self-policing mechanisms inherent in democratic institutions.

The second common thread is this: Our explanatory variables measure success in devising cooperative solutions to problems of collective action. Individuals can do little by themselves to maintain a stable currency, safeguard property rights, or establish fair and independent judiciaries. Cooperative effort is required, which on a national scale usually involves action at the level of government. Governments can enforce contracts. Governments can title property and protect it against seizure. Establishing and maintaining a democracy with its system of guaranteed political rights, civil liberties, and press freedoms is itself a constant collective-action effort.

Ours is a happy message. We did not dream of it when we began this study. Political freedom is and should be highly desired for its own sake by people everywhere on this earth. But there is icing on the cake: Freedom and democracy have happy spillover effects that bring economic prosperity and eventual wealth. What could be better?

Table A.2 Political events

COUNTRY	YEAR	DEMOCRATIC EVENT	YEAR	ANTI-DEMOCRATIC EVENT
Algeria			1991	Army suspends elections
Angola			1974	Independence & civil war
Bangladesh	1991	Transition to democracy	1971	Creation & one-party rule est'd.
Benin	1991	Free elections held	1974	Socialist state est'd.

Table A.2   Political events *(Continued)*

COUNTRY	YEAR	DEMOCRATIC EVENT	YEAR	ANTI-DEMOCRATIC EVENT
Bolivia	1981	Democratic civilian rule est'd.		
Botswana	1966	Independence		
Cape Verde	1991	Democratic reform	1975	Marxist, one-party rule est'd.
Central African Republic	1993	Civilian government installed	1960	Independence & rule by military dictatorship
Chad			1960	Independence & ethnic warfare
Chile	1990	Freely-elected presidency	1973	Pinochet dictatorship
Cuba			1959	Castro's repressive revolution
Dominican Republic	1996	Free & open elections		
Egypt			1947	Full sovereignty & one party rule
El Salvador	1992	Treaty signed for military & political reforms		
Gabon			1960	Autocratic presidents after independence
Ghana	1992	New constitution & multiparty elections	1957	Independence & series of military coups
Greece	1974	End of military rule & king; free elections		
Guatemala	1986	Civilian multi-party rule est'd.		
Haiti	1994	Aristide ends military rule		
Honduras	1980	Transition to democracy		
Indonesia	1999	First free elections in decades	1949	Independence & one party rule

Table A.2 Political events *(Continued)*

COUNTRY	YEAR	DEMOCRATIC EVENT	YEAR	ANTI-DEMOCRATIC EVENT
Ivory Coast			1999	Military coup
Kenya			1969	One party rule est'd.
Korea, South	1987	Democracy est'd.	1961	Authoritarian coup by Park Chung Hee
Lebanon	1991	Ends civil war & regains sovereignty		
Madagascar	1992	Free presidential & Assembly elections	1975	Single-party rule
Malaysia	1963	Malaysia created independently	1969	Suspension of democracy
Mali	1992	First democratic elections & end of dictatorship	1960	Independence & dictatorship
Mauritania			1960	Independence & one party rule
Mauritius	1968	Independence		
Mongolia	1993	Ex-communists yield monopoly power		
Morocco			1956	Establishment of authoritarian regime
Mozambique	1990	Elections & end of communism	1975	Independence & communist rule
Myanmar			1962	Military junta est'd.
Namibia	1990	Independence		
Nepal	1990	Multiparty democracy est'd.		
Nicaragua	1990	Transition to democracy		
Niger	1999	Civilian rule est'd.	1960	Independence, but no free elections
Nigeria	1999	New constitution & civilian rule est'd.	1983	Military rule commences
Nigeria II	1960	Independence under democracy	1966	Military coup
Pakistan	1988	Democratic transition	1999	Military takeover

Table A.2 Political events *(Continued)*

COUNTRY	YEAR	DEMOCRATIC EVENT	YEAR	ANTI-DEMOCRATIC EVENT
Panama	1989	Dictator Noriega deposed	1968	Dictatorship est'd.
Paraguay	1989	Free & regular presidential elections begin	1954	Stroessner dictatorship est'd.
Peru	1980	Democracy returns	1968	Military rule commences
Philippines, The	1986	Dictator Marcos forced into exile	1972	Marcos declares martial law
Portugal	1974	Broad democratic reforms installed		
Rwanda	1999	First local elections	1956	Ethnic warfare & removal of king
Singapore	1965	Independence		
Somalia			1969	Military dictatorship est'd.
South Africa	1994	End to apartheid		
Sudan			1956	Independence & military dictatorships
Sudan II			1989	Military coup
Syria			1949	Series of military coups commences
Taiwan	1992	Multi-party rule est'd.	1949	KMT establishes one-party rule
Tanzania	1995	First democratic elections since 1970s	1972	One party rule est'd.
Togo			1967	Military ruler est'd.
Trinidad & Tobago	1962	Independence		
Tunisia			1956	Independence & one-party state est'd.
Uganda			1966	Dictatorial regime est'd.

Table A.2 Political events *(Continued)*

Country	Year	Democratic Event	Year	Anti-democratic Event
Uruguay	1985	Civilian rule restored	1973	Military rule est'd.
Venezuela	1959	Democratically elected government ends military rule		
Zambia	1991	Elections & end of one-party rule	1964	Independence & one party rule

Notes

The authors are grateful for constructive comments and suggestions from Jagdish Bhagwati, Eric de Bodt, Alfredo Eisenberg, Milton Friedman, Dominique Hanssens, Ross Levine, Sebastian Edwards, Ed Leamer, Steven Lippman, Alan Meltzer, Larry Press, Robert Putnam, Dani Rodrik, Stephen Ross, David Rothman, Zane Spindler, and Avanidhar Subrahmanyam. Daron Acemoglu pointed us to some very useful historical data for which we are deeply grateful. Comments on this article are welcome and may be sent to the authors at *rroll@anderson.ucla.edu* and *johntalbs@hotmail.com*.

[1] Growth rates within each country vary considerably from year to year, or even within the same year. This inherent noise masks the correlation of growth with even strong explanatory variables. See William Easterly, Michael Kremer, Lant Pritchett, and Lawrence Summers, "Good Policy or Good Luck? Country Growth Performance and Temporary Shocks," *Journal of Monetary Economics* 32 (December 1993): 459–483. Moreover, many countries, especially developing countries, do not always report economic statistics in a timely or accurate way. Time slippage between the dependent and independent variables attenuates any correlation that might otherwise be observed. Big, successful, wealthy, developed countries just do not grow that fast in percentage terms. They have more critical mass to move, which makes big exponential growth difficult. In the past, they implemented structural changes that led to successful development; their growth spurts are behind them. Finally, the hundreds of potential explanatory variables that have been tested to date may be highly correlated with each other, making true determinations of a

possible relation with the dependent variable difficult. It is for this reason that we utilize Principal Components Analysis in our statistical approach.

[2] These sources are the *CIA World Factbook* (*www.cia.gov/cia/publications/ factbook/*); the Heritage Foundation's "Index of Economic Freedom"; the scores on political rights, civil liberties, and press freedom put out annually by Freedom House; per capita income figures from both the World Bank and Angus Maddison, *The World Economy: A Millenial Perspective*. (Paris: Development Centre of the Organization for Economic Cooperation and Development, 2001.) In working with the data, we used nonlinear transformations of the basic variables because we lacked an *a priori* opinion about functional form. We used standard econometric methods to control for substantial cross-correlations among some of these variables.

[3] For the statistically minded, the 81 to 85 percent figures are the adjusted R-squares in cross-country multiple regressions and the "significant" variables have t-statistics ranging (in absolute value) between two and twelve.

[4] Friedman, Milton, *Capitalism and Freedom* (Chicago: University of Chicago Press, 1962).

[5] We describe our data in Tables 1 and 2 at *www.anderson.ucla.edu/acad_unit/ finance/wp/2001/19-01.pdf*. All these data are available at the websites of the individual sources. Detailed regression results are given in Table 5 on the websites along with the countries included each year. Many variables actually exceed a 99 percent level of significance.

[6] William R. Easterly, *The Elusive Quest for Growth: Economists' Adventures and Misadventures in the Tropics* (Cambridge: MIT Press 2001.)

[7] Hernando de Soto, *The Mystery of Capital: Why Capitalism Triumphs in the West and Fails Everywhere Else* (New York: Basic, 2000): 6–7.

[8] Hernando de Soto, *The Other Path: The Invisible Revolution in the Third World* (New York: Harper and Row, 1989.)

[9] Hernando de Soto, *The Mystery of Capital*, 35.

[10] Rafael La Porta, Florencio Lopez-de-Silanes, Andrei Shleifer, and Robert Vishny, "The Quality of Government," National Bureau of Economic Research Working Paper 6727, September 1998.

[11] William J. Talbott, *Why Human Rights Should Be Universal*. (Oxford University Press, forthcoming, 2004).

[12] Amartya Sen, *Poverty and Famines: An Essay on Entitlement and Deprivation* (New York: Oxford University Press, 1981).

[13] Robert E. Hall and Charles I. Jones, "Why Do Some Countries Produce So Much More Output Per Worker Than Others?" *Quarterly Journal of Economics* 114.1 (February 1999): 83–116.

[14] For a thoughtful survey of the "democratic-peace thesis" and the issues surrounding it, see James Lee Ray, "The Democratic Path to Peace," *Journal of Democracy* 8 (April 1997): 49–64.

[15] William J. Talbott, *Why Human Rights Should Be Universal.*

[16] Jeffrey D. Sachs and Andrew M. Warner, "Economic Reform and the Process of Global Integration," *Brookings Papers on Economic Activity* 95.1 (1995): 1–95.

[17] Using 1999 data, a simple bivariate regression of GNIpc on trade levels (measured as exports as a percentage of GDP) has an adjusted R-square of 6.5 percent and a t-statistic of 3.26 (139 countries). But when the trade variable is added as another regressor in our multivariate model, its t-statistic is −1.03 (134 countries). The coefficient is negative and insignificant, so it seems doubtful that a country can export its way to growth.

[18] E.L. Fama, L. Fisher, M. Jensen, and R. Roll, "The Adjustment of Stock Prices to New Information," *International Economic Review* 10 (February 1969): 1–21.

[19] The results of our search are sorted by event type and country in Table 6, viewable in the online version of this essay and are reported in summary form as Table A.2 to this article. GNIpc come from Angus Maddison, who has compiled them over at least the last 50 years. All GNI data are reported in 1990 Geary-Khamis constant international dollars. In collecting the sample of events, we included all identifiable countries that reported data without any consideration whatsoever of their historical patterns of income. The event study approach lines up countries by date *relative* to the event date, which in our case is denoted as Year 0. GNIpc for each country was tabulated from ten years before the event to 20 years after, whenever possible. However, three decades of data are not always available, often because the event happened recently, or too soon after GNI data became available. In some instances, the country simply failed to report GNI in one or more years.

Each country's GNIpc data were used to compute year-to-year percentage changes relative to the event year (Year 0). This allows us to take cross-country averages of percentage changes each relative year thereby weighting countries equally, regardless of their initial state of prosperity. It also permits the depiction of a typical GNIpc pattern over all three decades even though some countries are missing data for a portion of this time period. To depict the time path of GNIpc, we first linked growth rate relatives before and after Year 0, then rescaled the resulting numbers so that GNIpc is the actual cross-country average in Year 0. The result appears as Figure A.1. Table 7 in the online version of this essay reports average annual growth rates of GNIpc and provides formal tests of statistical significance.

REFERENCES

Acemoglu, Daron, Simon Johnson and James A. Robinson. 2001. "The Colonial Origins of Comparative Development: An Empirical Investigation." *American Economic Review* 91 (December) 1369–1401.

_____. 2002. "Reversal of Fortune: Geography and Institutions in the Making of the Modern World Income Distribution." *Quarterly Journal of Economics* 117 (November), 1231–1294.

Alesina, Alberto, and Dani Rodrik. 1994. "Distributive Politics and Economic Growth." *Quarterly Journal of Economics* 109 (May), 465–490.

Aron, Janine. 2000. "Growth and Institutions, A Review of the Evidence." *The World Bank Research Observer* 15, 1 (February) 99–135.

Barro, Robert J. 1991. "Economic Growth in a Cross-Section of Countries." *Quarterly Journal of Economics* 106, 2 (May), 407–443.

_____. 1996. "Democracy and Growth." *Journal of Economic Growth* 1, 1, 1–27.

Becker, Gary. 1983. "A Theory of Competition Among Pressure Groups for Political Influence." *Quarterly Journal of Economics* 98, 371–400.

Bhagwati, Jagdish. 1988. "Export-Promoting Trade Strategy: Issues and Evidence." *The World Bank Research Observer* 3, 1, (January), 27–57.

Birdsall, Nancy, and Juan Luis Londono. 1997. "Asset Inequality Matters: An Assessment of the World Bank's Approach to Poverty Reduction." *American Economic Review* 87, 2 (May), 32–37.

Bok, Derek. 2003. *Universities in the Marketplace : The Commercialization of Higher Education.* Princeton, NJ: Princeton University Press.

Brunetti, Aymo, Gregory Kisunko, and Beatrice Weder. 1998. "Credibility of Rules and Economic Growth: Evidence from a Worldwide Survey of the Private Sector." *The World Bank Economic Review* 12, 3, 353–384.

Central Intelligence Agency. 2003. *CIA World Factbook.* Washington, D. C.: Central Intelligence Agency; Supplier of Documents.

Clague, Christopher, Philip Keefer, Stephen Knack, and Mancur Olsen. 1995. "Contract-Intensive Money: Contract Enforcement, Property Rights, and Economic Performance." Economics Department, University of Maryland, College Park.

_____. 1996. "Property and Contract Rights in Autocracies and Democracies." *Journal of Economic Growth* 1, 2 (June), 243–276.

Dawson, John W. 1998. "Institutions, Investment, and Growth: New Cross-Country and Panel Data Evidence." *Economic Inquiry* 36, 4, 603–619.

De Soto, Hernando. 1989. *The Other Path*: *The Invisible Revolution in the Third World.* New York: Harper and Row.

_____. 2000. *The Mystery of Capital. Why Capitalism Triumphs in the West and Fails Everywhere Else.* New York: Basic Books—Perseus Books Group.

De Vanssay, Xavier, and Zane A. Spindler. 1992. "Freedom and Growth: Do Constitutions Matter?" Economics Department, Simon Fraser University, Vancouver, B. C., Canada.

Diamond, Larry. 1992. *Globalization of Democracy: Trends, Types, Causes, and Prospects.* Abuja, Nigeria: Published for the Centre for Democratic Studies by Fena Typesetters and Graphics.

_____. 1999. *Developing Democracy: Toward Consolidation.* Baltimore: Johns Hopkins University Press.

Easterly, Willliam R. 2001. *The Elusive Quest for Growth: Economists' Adventures and Misadventures in the Tropics.* Cambridge, MA: MIT Press 2001.

Easterly, William, Michael Kremer, Lant Pritchett, and Lawrence Summers. 1993. "Good Policy or Good Luck? Country Growth Performance and Temporary Shocks." *Journal of Monetary Economics* 32 (December), 459–483.

Fama, E., L. Fisher, M. Jensen, and R. Roll. 1969. "The Adjustment of Stock Prices to New Information." *International Economic Review*, 10, 1 (February), 1–21.

Forbes, Kristin J., 2000, "A Reassessment of the Relationship Between Inequality and Growth," *American Economic Review* 90, 4 (September), 869–887.

Frankel, Jeffrey A. and David Romer. 1999. "Does Trade Cause Growth?" *The American Economic Review* 89, 3 (June), 379–399.

Friedman, Milton. 1962. *Capitalism and Freedom.* Chicago, IL: University of Chicago Press.

_____. 1963. *Monetary History of the United States 1867–1960.* New York: Princeton University Press.

Goldberg, Bernard. 2003. *Bias: A CBS Insider Exposes How the Media Distort the News.* New York: Perennial Books.

Goldsmith, Arthur A. 1995. "Democracy, Property Rights, and Economic Growth." *The Journal of Development Studies* 32, 2 (December), 157–174.

Greider, William. 1992. *Who Will Tell The People? The Betrayal of American Democracy.* New York: Simon & Schuster.

_____. 1997. *One World, Ready or Not: The Manic Logic of Global Capitalism.* New York: Simon & Schuster.

Hall, Robert E., and Charles I. Jones. 1999. "Why Do Some Countries Produce So Much More Output per Worker than Others?" *Quarterly Journal of Economics* (February).

Helliwell, John F. 1994. "Empirical Linkages Between Democracy and Economic Growth." *British Journal of Political Science* 24, 2 (April), 225–248.

Helliwell, John F., and Robert Putnam. 1995. "Social Capital and Economic Growth in Italy." *Eastern Economic Journal* 21, 3, 295–307.

Hillman, Amy J. and Gerald D. Keim. 2001. "Shareholder Value, Stakeholder Management, and Social Issues." *Strategic Management Journal* 22, 2 125–140.

Hirschman, Albert O. 1977. *The Passions and the Interests: Political Arguments for Capitalism Before Its Triumph.* Princeton, NJ: Princeton University Press.

Isham, Jonathan, Daniel Kaufmann, and Lant Pritchett. 1997. "Civil Liberties, Democracy, and the Performance of Government Projects." *The World Bank Economic Review* 11, 2, 219–242.

Kingsworth, Paul. 2003. *One No, Many Yeses—A Journey to the Heart of the Global Resistance Movement.* London: Simon and Schuster UK Ltd.

Knack, Stephen. 1996. "Institutions and the Convergence Hypothesis: The Cross-National Evidence." *Public Choice* 87 (3–4), 207–228.

Knack, Stephen, and Philip Keefer. 1995. "Institutions and Economic Performance: Cross-Country Tests Using Alternative Institutional Measures." *Economics and Politics* 7 (3), 207–227.

_____. 1997a. "Why Don't Poor Countries Catch Up? A Cross-National Test of an Institutional Explanation." *Economic Inquiry* 35 (July), 590–602.

_____. 1997b. "Does Social Capital Have an Economic Payoff? A Cross-Country Investigation." *Quarterly Journal of Economics* 112, 4 (November), 1251–1288.

Kormendi, Roger C., and Philip G. Meguire. 1985. "Macroeconomic Determinants of Growth: Cross-Country Evidence." *Journal of Monetary Economics* 16, 2 (September), 141–163.

Kotlikoff, Laurence J. 2001. "The Coming Generational Storm." Working Paper. *The National Bureau of Economics Research.*

Krugman, Paul. 2003. *The Great Unraveling—Losing Our Way in the New Century.* New York: W.W. Norton.

Kuznets, Simon. 1955. "Economic Growth and Income Inequality." *American Economic Review* 45,1 (March), 1–28.

La Porta, Rafael, Florencio Lopez-de-Silanes, Andrei Shleifer, and Robert Vishny. 1999. "The Quality of Government." *Journal of Law, Economics and Organization* 15, 222–279.

Levine, Ross, and David Renelt. 1992. "A Sensitivity Analysis of Cross-Country Regressions." *American Economic Review* 82, 4 (September), 942–963.

Maddison, Angus. 2001. *The World Economy: A Millennial Perspective.* Paris, France: Development Centre of the Organization for Economic Cooperation and Development.

Mankiw, N. Gregory, David Romer, and David N. Weil. 1992. "A Contribution to the Empirics of Economic Growth." *Quarterly Journal of Economics*, (May), 407–437.

Marcos, Subcomandante Insurgente. 2001. *Our Word Is Our Weapon.* New York: Seven Stories Press.

Mauro, Paolo. 1995. "Corruption and Growth." *Quarterly Journal of Economics* 110, 3 (August), 681–712.

McChesney, Robert W. 2000. *Rich Media, Poor Democracy.* New York: The New Press/W.W. Norton.

Mills, John Stuart. 2003. *On Liberty.* New Haven, Conn: Yale University Press.

Moore, Michael. 2001. *Stupid White Men.* New York: Harper Collins.

Murphy, Kevin M., Andrei Shleifer, and Robert W. Vishny. 1991. "The Allocation of Talent: Implications for Growth." *Quarterly Journal of Economics* 106, 2 (May), 503–530.

Ng, Francis, and Alexander Yeats. 1999. "Good Governance and Trade Policy: Are They the Keys to Africa's Global Integration and Growth?" Trade Research Team, World Bank, Washington, D. C.

Olson, Mancur. 1971. *The Logic of Collective Action: Public Goods and the Theory of Groups.* Cambridge, Mass: Harvard University Press.

_____. 1986, Why Some Welfare-State Redistribution to the Poor Is a Great Idea, in Charles K. Rowley, ed., *Public Choice and Liberty: Essays in Honor of Gordon Tullock*, (Oxford: Basil Blackwell).

Palast, Greg. 2002. *The Best Democracy Money Can Buy.* New York: Pluto Press.

Perotti, Roberto. 1996. "Growth, Income Distribution, and Democracy: What the Data Say." *Journal of Economic Growth* 1 (June), 149–187.

Persson, Torsten, and Guido Tabellini. 1994. "Is Inequality Harmful for Growth? Theory and Evidence." *American Economic Review* 84, 3 (June), 600–621.

Powell, Jim. 2003. *FDR's Folly: How Roosevelt and His New Deal Prolonged the Great Depression.* New York: Crown Forum.

Przeworski, Adam, and Fernando Limongi. 1993. "Political Regimes and Economic Growth." *Journal of Economic Perspectives* 7, 3, 51–69.

Putnam, Robert. 2001. *Bowling Alone: The Collapse and Revival of American Community.* New York: Simon & Schuster.

Rajan, Raghuram G. and Luigi Zingales. 2003. *Saving Capitalism from the Capitalists.* New York: Crown Business/Random House.

Rodrik, Dani. 2001. "Institutions, Integration, and Geography: In Search of the Deep Determinants of Economic Growth." Center for International Development, John F. Kennedy School of Government, Harvard University (September).

Roll, Richard, and John Talbott. 2002. "The End of Class Warfare: An Examination of Income Disparity." Working paper. On http://www.anderson.ucla.edu/acad_unit/finance/wp/2002/5-02.pdf. (April).

_____. 2003. "Political Freedom, Economic Liberty, and Prosperity." *Journal of Democracy.* 14, 3 (July), 75–89. (A reprint of this article is included as an appendix to this book).

Sachs, Jeffrey D., and Andrew M. Warner. 1995. "Economic Reform and the Process of Global Integration." *Brookings Papers on Economic Activity 95,* 1, 1–118.

_____. 2000 "Natural Resource Abundance and Economic Growth." *Leading Issues in Economic Development.* New York: Oxford University Press.

Sala-i-Martin, Xavier. 1997. "I Just Ran Two Million Regressions," *American Economic Review* 87, 2, (May), 178–183.

Savage, Michael. 2003. The Savage Nation: Saving America from the Liberal Assault on Our Borders, Language and Culture. Nashville, Tenn: Thomas Nelson Publishers.

Scully, Gerald W. 1988. "The Institutional Framework and Economic Development." *Journal of Political Economy* 96, 3, 652–662.

Sen, Amartya Kumar. 1981. *Poverty and Famines: An Essay on Entitlement and Deprivation.* New York: Oxford University Press.

_____. 1999. *Development as Freedom.* New York: Knopf Publishing/Random House.

Shleifer, Andrei, E. Glaeser, and J. Scheinkman. 2003. "The Injustice of Inequality." *Journal of Monetary Economics: Carnegie-Rochester Series on Public Policy, (January).*

Smith, Adam. 1776. *The Wealth of Nations.* Edited by Edwin Cannan. 1994. New York: Modern Library.

Soley, Lawrence C. 1995. *Leasing the Ivory Tower: The Corporate Takeover of Academia.* Boston, Mass: South End Press.

Solow, Robert. 1956. "A Contribution to the Theory of Economic Growth." *Quarterly Journal of Economics*, (February).

Spindler, Zane. 1991. "Liberty and Development: A Further Empirical Perspective." *Public Choice* 69, (February), 197–210.

Stigler, George. 1971. "Theory of Economic Regulation." *Bell Journal of Economics and Management Science* 2, 3–21.

Stiglitz, Joseph E. 2002. *Globalization and Its Discontents*. New York: W.W. Norton.

Talbott, John. 2003. *The Coming Crash of the Housing Market*. New York: McGraw-Hill.

Talbott, William J. 2004. *Why Human Rights Should Be Universal*. Oxford University Press, (forthcoming). Excerpts currently available at http://faculty.washington.edu/wtalbott/rights/talbott.htm.

INDEX

FINANCIAL TIMES PRENTICE HALL BOOKS

For more information, please go to www.ft-ph.com

Business and Society

Douglas K. Smith
On Value and Values: Thinking Differently About We in an Age of Me

Current Events

Alan Elsner
Gates of Injustice: The Crisis in America's Prisons

John R. Talbott
Where America Went Wrong: And How to Regain Her Democratic Ideals

Economics

David Dranove
*What's Your Life Worth? Health Care Rationing...Who Lives? Who Dies?
Who Decides?*

Entrepreneurship

Dr. Candida Brush, Dr. Nancy M. Carter, Dr. Elizabeth Gatewood,
Dr. Patricia G. Greene, and Dr. Myra M. Hart
Clearing the Hurdles: Women Building High Growth Businesses

Oren Fuerst and Uri Geiger
*From Concept to Wall Street: A Complete Guide to Entrepreneurship
and Venture Capital*

David Gladstone and Laura Gladstone
*Venture Capital Handbook: An Entrepreneur's Guide to Raising Venture Capital,
Revised and Updated*

Thomas K. McKnight
*Will It Fly? How to Know if Your New Business Idea Has Wings...
Before You Take the Leap*

Stephen Spinelli, Jr., Robert M. Rosenberg, and Sue Birley
Franchising: Pathway to Wealth Creation

Executive Skills

Cyndi Maxey and Jill Bremer
It's Your Move: Dealing Yourself the Best Cards in Life and Work

John Putzier
Weirdos in the Workplace

Finance

Aswath Damodaran
*The Dark Side of Valuation: Valuing Old Tech, New Tech, and New
Economy Companies*

Kenneth R. Ferris and Barbara S. Pécherot Petitt
Valuation: Avoiding the Winner's Curse

International Business and Globalization

John C. Edmunds
Brave New Wealthy World: Winning the Struggle for World Prosperity

Robert A. Isaak
The Globalization Gap: How the Rich Get Richer and the Poor Get Left Further Behind

Johny K. Johansson
In Your Face: How American Marketing Excess Fuels Anti-Americanism

Peter Marber
Money Changes Everything: How Global Prosperity Is Reshaping Our Needs, Values, and Lifestyles

Fernando Robles, Françoise Simon, and Jerry Haar
Winning Strategies for the New Latin Markets

Investments

Zvi Bodie and Michael J. Clowes
Worry-Free Investing: A Safe Approach to Achieving Your Lifetime Goals

Michael Covel
Trend Following: How Great Traders Make Millions in Up or Down Markets

Aswath Damodaran
Investment Fables: Exposing the Myths of "Can't Miss" Investment Strategies

Harry Domash
Fire Your Stock Analyst! Analyzing Stocks on Your Own

David Gladstone and Laura Gladstone
Venture Capital Investing: The Complete Handbook for Investing in Businesses for Outstanding Profits

D. Quinn Mills
Buy, Lie, and Sell High: How Investors Lost Out on Enron and the Internet Bubble

D. Quinn Mills
Wheel, Deal, and Steal: Deceptive Accounting, Deceitful CEOs, and Ineffective Reforms

H. David Sherman, S. David Young, and Harris Collingwood
Profits You Can Trust: Spotting & Surviving Accounting Landmines

Leadership

Jim Despain and Jane Bodman Converse
And Dignity for All: Unlocking Greatness through Values-Based Leadership

Marshall Goldsmith, Cathy Greenberg, Alastair Robertson, and Maya Hu-Chan
Global Leadership: The Next Generation

Management

Rob Austin and Lee Devin
Artful Making: What Managers Need to Know About How Artists Work

J. Stewart Black and Hal B. Gregersen
Leading Strategic Change: Breaking Through the Brain Barrier

David M. Carter and Darren Rovell
On the Ball: What You Can Learn About Business from Sports Leaders

Charles J. Fombrun and Cees B.M. Van Riel
Fame and Fortune: How Successful Companies Build Winning Reputations

Personal Finance

David Shapiro
Retirement Countdown: Take Action Now to Get the Life You Want

Steve Weisman
A Guide to Elder Planning: Everything You Need to Know to Protect Yourself Legally and Financially

Strategy

Edward W. Davis and Robert E. Spekmam
The Extended Enterprise: Gaining Competitive Advantage through Collaborative Supply Chains

Joel M. Shulman, With Thomas T. Stallkamp
Getting Bigger by Growing Smaller: A New Growth Model for Corporate America

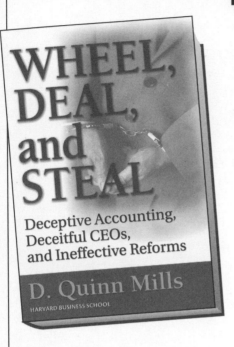